The POETS *of*
MODERN FRANCE

The POETS *of*
MODERN FRANCE

by

LUDWIG LEWISOHN

KENNIKAT PRESS
Port Washington, N. Y./London

THE POETS OF MODERN FRANCE

First published in 1918
Reissued in 1970 by Kennikat Press
Library of Congress Catalog Card No: 78-103231
SBN 8046-0868-7

Manufactured by Taylor Publishing Company   Dallas, Texas

PREFACE

Iᴛ is time that the art of translation, of which we have many beautiful examples in English, should be strictly distinguished from the trade. Like acting or the playing of music, it is an art of interpretation, more difficult than either in this respect: that you must interpret your original in a medium never contemplated by its author. It requires, at its best, an exacting and imaginative scholarship, for you must understand your text in its fullest and most living sense; it requires a power over the instrument of your own language no less complete than the virtuoso's over the pianoforte, than the actor's over the expression of his voice or the gestures of his body. Its aim, too, is identical with the aims of those sister arts of interpretation: to give a clear voice to beauty that would else be dumb or quite muffled. For even to intelligent lovers of the arts a subtle or intricate poem in a language not their own is as lifeless as a page of Beethoven which they have not heard played.

What now should be the aim of the translator of poetry? For it is with poetry that I am here concerned. It should be clearly, first of all, to produce a beautiful poem. If he has not done that he may have served the cause of information, of language study. In art he has committed a plain ineptitude. If he has produced a beautiful poem, much should be forgiven him, although a beautiful poem may not, necessarily, be a beautiful translation. To be that it must sustain certain relations to its original. It must, to begin with, be faithful—not pedantically, but essentially, not only to the general content of the original poem but to its specific means of embodying that content. There should be as little definite alteration, addition or omission as possible. In the translations in this volume there will not be found, I think, more than a dozen words that were not in the texts, or more than half a dozen actual verbal substitutions. The associative values of two different linguistic media should, of course, be sensitively borne in mind. One idiom must be made not only to copy but rightly to interpret the other. It is better, however, to risk a slight obscurity which time and the growth of new artistic insights may remove than to substitute an easy meaning for your author's troublesome one.

The second relation which the translated poem must sustain to its original concerns the far more difficult and exacting matter of form. The language involved will, of course, modify the character of the translator's problem. If he is dealing with languages that have practically the same prosodic system, any two Germanic languages for instance, he must scrupulously preserve the music, the exact cadences of his original. If he is translating from a language that has a quite different prosody, such as the French, he must interpret the original forms by analogous forms. Thus I have rendered all poems written wholly in alexandrines into English heroic verse, but I have sought to make that verse as fluid and as various in movement as the types of alexandrine in my originals. When the prosodic contour of a poem, however, depended definitely upon the contrast of alexandrines with longer or shorter verses, I have preserved the exact syllabic lengths. In lyrical measures the aim must be, of course, to hear the characteristic music, to transfer this and to follow its modulations from line to line and stanza to stanza.

But these are only the external properties of form. What characterises a poet, above all else, is the way he uses his medium, his precise and unique method of moulding his language—in respect both of diction and rhythm—for the expression of his personal sense of life. It is here that the translator comes upon his hardest task. For he should try, hopeless as that may seem, to use his medium of speech in a given translation even as the original poet used his own. The translated poem, in brief, should be such as the original poet would have written if the translator's language had been his native one.

I am quite aware that, in the sixty translated poems in this volume, I have not always even approached my own ideal of what a translation of poetry should be.   But to have attempted the task upon such principles may, of itself, not be without service to the practice of the art.

For my critical introduction on the poets of modern France I have no such apology to make. Critics of power and place have told me repeatedly how wrong-headed my critical method is.   Let me remind them, who know it so much better than I, of the history of literature and of criticism. For if that history makes but one thing admirably and indisputably clear it is this: In every age the New Poetry and the New Criticism have prevailed in so far as they produced excellent work according to their own intentions and in harmony with their own aims.   In every age the critical conservatives have protested in the name of eternal principles which, alas, are not eternal at all.   And generally, for such is human nature, the innovators in art and thought of one generation, of one decade at times, have become the conservatives of the next.   In another ten or fifteen years I may myself be frowning upon a still newer criticism, a still newer art. . . . But today I am in the right,

not of my own desert, but through the ways of
the World Spirit. . . .

Ludwig Lewisohn.

New York City,
   January, 1918.

CONTENTS

[xiii]

[xiv]

INTRODUCTION

INTRODUCTION

I

THE SOURCES OF THE NEW POETRY

Le Poète doit être le maître
absolu des formes de la Vie, et non
en être l'esclave comme les Réalistes
et les Naturalistes.

STUART MERRILL

THE struggle of man, however blind and stumbling, however checked by tribal rage and tribal terror, is toward self-hood. This truth is superficially assented to, it has become a glib commonplace to the sociologist: it has really penetrated only a few rare and lonely minds. The majority, simple and learned, talks of individualism and cries out upon the plainest implications of its own doctrine. Not only in life, but also in art. Yet the history of literature, and especially of poetry, illustrates nothing in the history of the mind more

[1]

clearly than this: the pang of beauty, the exaltation in truth, the vision of the tragedy of life arise, in the fullest sense, only when the individual liberates himself from the tribe and faces the universe alone. Tribal lays, still largely communal in diction and metre, receive—as in the Odyssey or the Nibelungenlied—an immortal accent from the voice of a nameless personal redactor and the rude legends of the Latian tribe from the melancholy beauty of Vergil's soul. The metrical romances of the Middle Ages, on the contrary, are scarcely distinguishable one from the other, and even so cultivated an age as the Renaissance illustrates in its faded sonnet-cycles the dominance of a tribal convention. Such verse becomes strangely hushed and inarticulate in the course of time. We listen for the voice of a man and hear the murmur of the tribe. . . .

It is, in poetry, chiefly a matter of form, of music. The tribal verse-chant is rigid in character and the minstrels are more than nameless, they are, in the personal sense, voiceless. The philologist's speculations in regard to authorship remain mere speculations. There is very little of

[2]

the personal note in the older poetry of Europe, North or South. Even when notable personalities gradually emerge—Dante, Walther von der Vogelweide, Chaucer, Villon — the humbler singers still remain the voices of the folk. The second stage of poetical form, the stage illustrated by all the great historic literatures, presents tradition modified by personality. The forms are limited in number and in character. But into each form the individual poet pours or tries to pour the unique music of his soul. That union of fixed form and personal accent is illustrated by the history of the hexameter in Latin, the alexandrine in French, the Spenserian stanza, blank verse and the heroic couplet in English poetry. And the conservative forces in modern poetry and criticism still point to this method—the traditional form modified by the personal accent—as the only sound and noble method of poetical creation. Such, in effect, is the essential view of the critic who will not look at "free verse" not because it is poor, but because it is "free," who, in another field, condemns the imaginative creations of a great dramatist for not being in a fixed and traditional

[3]

sense—plays. The echoes of this critic are all about us: "It's beautiful, but it isn't poetry!" "It's powerful, but it isn't a play!" As though, in some quite transcendental sense, there were a divine, Platonic, arch-typal idea of poetry, of drama, which it is the duty of the artist to seek, at least, to approach. In art, as in morals, as in state-craft, the timorous Absolutist clings to his Idea, his formula, as the permanent and abiding element in the flux of concrete things. He does not see that the abiding is in the trend to finer types, to freer and more personal kinds of self-realisation, is, in fact, in that dark angel of his dreams, man's will to change.

The last stage in the development of poetic form comes when, under the stress of the modern world, the poet's struggle toward the realisation of his self-hood becomes so keen that he cannot use the traditional forms any more at all. He must find his own form: his impulse is so new and strange that it must create its own music or be silent. Not because he does not love and revere the forms of the masters. But he cannot express himself through them; he cannot, to speak in a homely

[4]

way, turn around in them. They come trailing so much glory. And the glory is alien to his very urgent and immediate business. The very splendor of their associations, the throb of the music of a thousand voices, nobler, perhaps, than his, paralyse him. He is like a stripling running a race in the brocades of an ancient king. . . . Yet he must be himself or he is nothing or, at most, an echo. Such is the sound and legitimate reason for those experiments in free verse, in rhythmic and rimed prose, which have arisen in every fully equipped modern literature within the past twenty-five years. I must not say that thus a new and personal kind of truth in beauty has yet been quite achieved. But the impulse is right and necessary, and the aim the only one left to the modern poet. Hence while official criticism sits, as everywhere and always, amid the wreckage of its commandments and its prophecies, the poets of the modern world have gone forth in search of a new freedom and a new music.

I have spoken of the preceptist critic, the absolutist in criticism with his laws and formulæ antecedent to experience and to art which grows out of experience. But another kind of critic has appeared and has been heard. And one such, the late M. Rémy de Gourmont, has admirably summed up the whole matter: "The only excuse that a man has for writing is that he express his own self, that he reveal to others the kind of world that is reflected in his individual mirror: his only excuse is that he be original: he must say things not said before and say them in a form not formulated before. He must create his own æsthetic, —and we must admit as many æsthetics as there are original minds and judge them according to what they are and not according to what they are not."

In France, as elsewhere, the new poetry and the new criticism sprang from very deep sources in the life of the mind and corresponded with the larger tendencies of the new age. For the epoch since the Revolution may almost be divided—if every formula were not insufficient and a little empty— into three periods of struggle for the three kinds of liberty that we must attain: political, intellectual, moral. And in the history of French poetry three schools interpret closely and in right succession these three phases. To the Romantics of France, as to the Romantics of England (except Shelley) freedom was primarily an outer thing concerned with votes and governmental action: to the Parnassiens it was the right to observe the present and historic world objectively and let the reason draw its own sombre conclusions from that vision; to the Symbolists, the moderns, it is more; it is the right to complete realisation of one's selfhood—which includes and demands economic justice—in action and in art. It is that new idealism which, to quote Gourmont again, "means the free and personal development of the intellectual individual in the intellectual series."

These movements are general and European. One need adduce no external influence to account for their appearance in any of the great literary nations, least of all in the self-contained and self-sufficient intellectual life of France. Yet it seems very certain that the modern movement in French poetry drew a good deal of its deeper guidance from the one literature in which Romanticism had shown little if any interest in political liberty, but very much in that of personal conduct, of speculation and of art.   Here I may let M. de Gourmont speak once more: "In relation to man, the thinking subject, the world, all that is external to the I, exists only according to the idea of it which he shapes for himself.   We know only phenomena, we reason only concerning appearances: all truth in itself escapes us: the essence is unapproachable. It is this fact which Schopenhauer has popularised in his very clear and simple formula: the world is my representation."   The French Symbolists, in other words, drew their doctrine of freedom in life and art partly, at least, from the doctrine of the post-Kantian idealists.   The creative self that projects the vision of the universe stands above it and need not be bound by the shadows it has itself evoked.   The inner realities became the supreme realities: Maeterlinck translated the *Fragments* of Novalis; Verhaeren declared that the "immediate end of the poet is to express himself."   The emphasis placed upon the unique and creative self might possibly be attributed to the Flemish and hence Germanic temper of the Belgian poets. But during the crucial years of the Symbolist movement the same view was shared by the most purely Latin poets who used the French tongue. In his excellent monograph on Henri de Régnier, M. Jean de Gourmont speaks of this matter in unmistakable terms: "Symbolism was not, at first, a revolution, but an evolution called forth by the infiltration of new philosophical ideas. The theories of Kant, of Schopenhauer, of Hegel and Hartmann began to spread in France: the poets were fairly intoxicated by them." It is curious to note, in this connection, the omission of Fichte's name. But the young men of eighteen hundred and eighty-five were not exact students and thinkers. They simply found in the philosophy of a definite school and age a vision which accorded with their own innermost feeling concerning the new freedom that must be won for life and for its close and intimate expression in the art of poetry.

II

"En vérité il n'y a pas de prose : il y a
l'alphabet, et puis des vers plus ou moins
serrés, plus ou moins diffus."

STÉPHANE MALLARMÉ

"Le vers libre, au lieu d'être, comme
l'ancien vers, des lines de prose coupées
par des rimes régulières, doit exister
en lui-même par des allitérations de
voyelles et de consonnes parentes."

GUSTAVE KAHN

THE young men of eighteen hundred and eighty-five began, as was natural, by an energetic rebellion against the dominant school of poetry. That school, the Parnassien, cultivated, as everyone knows, objectivity of vision, sculpturesque fullness and perfection of form, a completely impersonal attitude. It had been practically if not officially founded when Gautier published his

[10]

Émaux et Camées in 1850, it had shown remarkable power of endurance; it was unshaken by the incomparable notes of pure lyricism with which Verlaine, since 1868, had modified his partial acceptance of its own technical standards. It counted among its adherents every first-rate talent that had come to maturity toward the middle of the nineteenth century, even, again with certain modifications, that of Charles Baudelaire. Its representative poet was Leconte de Lisle. And Leconte de Lisle was a great poet. It is easier to see that now than it was, perhaps, twenty years ago. The rich, sonorous verses of the *Poèmes antiques* and the *Poèmes barbares* seem still to march as with the ringing mail of an undefeated army. And in every mind that he has once impressed remain as permanent possessions those images in stone or bronze under skies of agate or drenched in radiance which he embodied in the clang and thunder of his verse. But there was little personal, little of his own mind, except that one proud and imperturbable gesture; his art was, after all, decoration, even though it raised the decorative to heroic dimensions. . . . The younger generation that wanted intimate, concrete truth, subtle and personal, not large and general, that wanted, in a word, not eloquence but lyricism, inevitably arose against him and his fellows—against the rather timid naturalism of François Coppée, against the glittering dexterity of Téodore de Banville, the expounder in practice and criticism of the Parnassien technique. The young poets of the time turned, among the men of their own land and speech, to one dead and two living writers: to Charles Baudelaire, Paul Verlaine and Stéphane Mallarmé.

It is true that in *Les Fleurs du Mal* (1857) Baudelaire's verse is as firmly and precisely moulded as any Parnassien's, his rimes are as sonorous, his stanzaic structure as exact. Only in the sweep and passionate speed of perhaps two pieces, *Le Balcon* and *Harmonie du soir*:

"Voici venir les temps où vibrant sur sa tige
Chaque fleur s'évapore ainsi qu'un encensoir..." [1]

is there a new cadence. His influence upon the

[1] Lord Alfred Douglas translates happily if freely:
"This is the hour when swinging in the breeze,
Each flower like a censor sheds its sweet . . ."

future was due to his substance: to the merciless revelation of himself, his stubborn assertion of his strange and morbid soul, his harsh summons to others to cast aside their masks of moral idealism and confess themselves his equals and his kin:

"Hypocrite lecteur—mon semblable—mon frère." [1]

It was due to his belief in the unexplored wealth of beauty and horror of the subjective self:

"Homme, nul n'a sondé le fond de tes abîmes . . ." [2]

And that is, in a very real sense, what the Symbolists, the moderns, set out to do. Finally, by some strange prevision, or else in a moment of imaginative caprice, he struck off in a single sonnet, *Correspondances* (which has been quoted again and again,) the subtlest doctrine of the Symbolists:

"La nature est un temple où de vivants piliers
Laissent parfois sortir des confuses paroles;
L'homme y passe à travers des forêts de symboles
Qui l'observent avec des regards familiers . . ." [3]

[1] "Hypocritical reader—my fellow—my brother!"
[2] "Man, no one has sounded the bottom of thy abysses."
[3] Nature is a temple wherein living colmuns sometimes let confused words escape; man wanders there across forests of symbols which observe him with familiar glances."

[13]

To capture these obscure but revealing hints—
that, too, was part of the symbolist programme.

But the influence of Baudelaire upon the living
poets of France was slight compared to that ex-
erted by one far stranger and far greater than himself, by Paul Verlaine (1844–1896). For Verlaine was not only almost their contemporary—
the wayward, childlike, mystical creature, giving
them, as on a memorable occasion he did to George
Moore, some divine sonnet scribbled in bed in a
fetid slum: he was also the purest lyrical singer
that France had ever known. The most musical
songs of the Romantics have a touch of self-con-
sciousness and eloquence compared to his. Perhaps an infusion of Northern blood (he was born
at Metz) gave him the soul of a minstrel and a
child; it left him Latin enough to be, with all his
unrestrained lyricism, a subtle, accomplished and
even learned technician. He mastered the Parnassien method in his youth and used it exquis-
itely. But even in the early and correct *Poèmes
saturniens* (1866) there is the unforgettable
Chanson d'Automne with its strange sob, with that
note of the ineffable, the beyond in human longing

and regret which French poetry had never, or
never, at least, so simply and piercingly heard.
Eight years later had come the *Romances sans
Paroles*, the highest point, probably, in Verlaine's
lyrical achievement, and again seven years later
Sagesse. But even in the days of his declining
power, in the collections published when the modern movement was fully under way—*Amour*
(1888), *Parallèlement* (1889)—he kept the marvellous gift of suddenly lifting the hearer of his
verse into an infinite of imaginative pathos:

"Mon pauvre enfant, ta voix dans le Bois de Bou-
    logne . . . " [1]

or of imaginative splendor:

"Et, ô ces voix d'enfants chantant dans la coupole." [2]

The infinite . . . ! In that word lies the secret
of Verlaine, of his difference from all the past of
French poetry, of his power over its present and
future. He does not exhaust his subject with the
glowing but appeasable passion of the Romantics;
he does not paint his vision in the hard, luminous

[1] "My poor child, thy voice in the Bois de Boulogne . . ."
[2] "And, O those children's voices singing in the cupola."

colors of the Parnassiens; he strikes a discreet and troubling note that leaves its vibrations in the heart and in the nerves forever.　His poetry, as he was well aware, withdrew deliberately from any relation to the plastic arts; it is full of images addressed to the ear; it seeks magic rather than beauty; it asks our tears rather than our admiration.　Words which the Parnassiens had used like the brilliant stone fragments of an Italian enameller were to Verlaine notes in the music of thought and passion; it is in this sense that he called his finest volume: *Songs Without Words*.　All this is, of course, merely saying that Verlaine is a lyrical poet of the type of Shelley or Heine.　But as such his achievement was quite new and revolutionary in the literature of France.

Less revolutionary was his influence upon form. He was bitter against the wrongs done by the Parnassiens in the name of rime; he protested against their sonorousness as he did against their brilliance —"*pas de couleur, rien que la nuance*"—he used the "*rythmes impairs*," verses of seven, eleven and thirteen syllables; he strove to make the music of verse subtler, more ductile, more quivering.　He cannot be said to have introduced any fundamental change. Yet everywhere among the modern poets is heard the music of those pale vowels of his, those trembling verses, as in the lines called *Menuet* which made the reputation of M. Fernand Gregh because they were mistaken for Verlaine's:

> "Chanson frêle du clavecin,
> Notes grêles, fuyant essaim
> Qui s'éfface . . . " [1]

The direct master of the moderns, however, and the acknowledged founder of the Symbolist school was Stéphane Mallarmé (1842–1898), a man of a very thin though very fine vein of authentic genius. His power over the younger men of his day was due not wholly, not even primarily, to his sheaf of mystical and undulating verse. He had reflected closely and deeply upon the sources of poetry and upon the nature of the poetic imagination; he communicated the results of his thought not only in his critical fragments but in exquisite monologues during those famous Tuesday evenings of his in the Rue de Rome which became an

[1] "Fragile song of the harpsichord, pale, sharp notes, a fleeing swarm that fades away . . ."

institution in the middle eighties. There gathered to be with him "in that drawing room faintly lit to which the shadowy corners gave the aspect of a temple and an oratory," and to hear his "seductive and lofty doctrine on poetry and art" Kahn and Ghil and Laforgue, Vielé-Griffin and Régnier, Stuart Merrill and Louys and Mauclair, John Payne and Arthur Symons and a group of lesser talents. "We passed unforgettable hours there," writes M. Albert Mockel, "the best, doubtless, that we shall ever know. . . . And he who made us welcome there was the absolute type of poet, the heart than can love, the brow that can understand, inferior to nothing, yet disdaining nothing, for he discerned in each thing a secret teaching or an image of Beauty." The tributes of the younger men who heard him thus form a small body of very beautiful writing and include noble verses of memorial or praise by Vielé-Griffin, by Louys and by Régnier. The latter describes in the fine dedicatory sonnet to *La Cité des Eaux* the external aims of other poets and then turns to Mallarmé:

"Mais vous, Maître, certain que toute gloire est nue,
Vous marchiez dans la vie et dans la vérité
Vers l'invisible étoile en vous-même apparue." [1]

I have tried elsewhere to give a close interpretation of the symbolist doctrine [2] which is permanently connected with the name of Mallarmé and has shaped not only the work of the maturer of the living poets of France but even that of the youngest among them. It comes, in plainest terms, to this: that the poet is to use the details of the phenomenal world exclusively as symbols of that inner or spiritual reality which it is his aim to project in art. In this there is, of course, nothing absolutely new. Poets, especially lyrical poets, have, as a matter of fact, always done that quite instinctively. Images drawn from the world which the senses perceive are our only means of communicating the nameless things of the inner life. What was and is relatively new in the doctrine and the practice of the Symbolists is their

1 "But you, Master, assured that all glory is bare, you trod the ways of life and truth toward that invisible star arisen in yourself."

2 *Vide:* LEWISOHN. *The Modern Drama* (Second Edition). Chapter V.

subtle and conscious cultivation of this method, their rejection (in the heat of the reaction against the Parnassiens) of the objective as utterly devoid of significance, of truth, even of existence; their search for the strange and mysterious, the unobserved and unheard of in the shifting visions of the world. . . . But I shall let Mallarmé speak briefly for himself: "To name an object is to suppress three-fourths of the delight of a poem which consists of the happiness of divining little by little; poetic vision arises from suggestion *(le suggérer voilà le rêve)*. It is the perfect use of this mystery which constitutes the symbol, to evoke little by little an object in order to show a state of soul, or, inversely, to disengage from it a state of soul by a series of decipherings." To this may be added a passage from the famous manifesto which Jean Moréas, in his symbolist days, published in *Le Figaro* (September 18, 1886): "Symbolist poetry seeks to clothe the idea in a sensible form which, nevertheless, shall not be its final end and aim, but shall merely serve to express the idea which remains subjective." In this sentence ap-

[20]

pears very clearly, so clearly as perhaps nowhere else, the Symbolist's reaction against naturalism in both art and thought, against the "heavy and the weary weight" of an objective world, its insistence upon the freedom of the creative soul. . . . Mallarmé's personal teaching and practice was, of course, more esoteric. He dreamed, like Wagner, whom Verlaine and all the Symbolists adored, of a synthesis of the arts. A poem was to partake of music, of the plastic arts, of philosophic thought. To each of his verses, in the excellent interpretation of M. Téodore de Wyzéwa, "he sought to attach several superimposed senses." Each was to be an image, a thought, a note of music—a fragment of that large and mystic harmony in which the thinker and the world he thinks are one. . . . It was all essentially, I repeat, a liberation from the scientific, the objective, the relentless reality of earth to which—in the doctrine of the Naturalists—our souls are in bondage; it was a reaction of personality, of the freedom and splendor of the inner self, it was, as I said in starting, the modern striving toward self-hood.

The new spirit of poetry demanded a new form. To the discovery of this new form Mallarmé had contributed rather less than even Verlaine. Both used, with whatever new cadences within the verse, with whatever new lightness and brightness of rime, the traditional methods of French prosody: an identical number of syllables in the corresponding lines of a given poem, the rigid alternation of masculine and femine rimes, a rather strict limitation in the number and character of stanzaic forms. From this description it is clear that the *vers libre* invented and cultivated by the Symbolists did not mean any extraordinary liberty of versification from the point of view of any prosody but that of France. To the poets of England and Germany an arbitrary or personal variation of line length, as in the Pindarics from Cowley on, entire freedom of riming, the building of quatrains on a single rime had been immemorial possessions. They had, in truth, long gone beyond the earliest innovations of the Symbolists. For neither Kahn, Laforgue nor Vielé-Griffin ever discarded rime wholly. But that had been done, to go back no farther, by Southey and Shelley, by

Goethe and Novalis, by Heine and Matthew Arnold. The early *vers libre*, then, was simply a flexible and rather undulating form of lyric or odic verse, following in its cadences the development, the rise and fall, of the poet's mood, furnishing in its swaying harmonies an orchestration to thought and passion. Lyrical pieces of this character are Verhaeren's *November* (xi), Régnier's *Scene at Dusk* (xix), Kahn's *Provençe* (xxviii), and Gourmont's *The Exile of Beauty*, (xxxiv).

"To whom, then," asks M. Rémy de Gourmont, "do we owe *vers libre?*" And he answers: "To Rimbaud whose *Illuminations* appeared in *La Vogue* in 1886, to Jules Laforgue who at the same period and in the same precious little review— which M. Kahn was editing—printed *Légende* and *Solo de Lune*, and, finally, to M. Kahn himself." It would seem, as a matter of fact, that the innovations of Rimbaud were slight and that Laforgue knew of M. Kahn's theories for many years. The latter's *Les Palais Nomades* (1887) was, in addition, the first actually published volume of *vers libre;* it made a great stir in both France and Belgium and was directly responsible for the prosodic development that continued with Vielé-Griffin's *Joies* (1889), with its significant preface, Régnier's *Poèmes anciens et romanesques* (1890), and Verhaeren's *Au bord de la route* (1891). No further innovations in French versification were made until quite recently, except by M. de Régnier when he almost though not quite abandoned rime in the charming *Odelettes* of his volume *Les Jeux rustiques et divins* (1897).

There is available, at least at present, no evidence of any direct foreign influence upon the rise of free verse in French poetry. Nor, were there such evidence, would I be willing to attach any significance to it. A great many sins have been committed by the scholarly search for influences. A saner and more philosophic view of the history of literature regards the appearance of new sources of inspiration and new forms of expression as outgrowths of those larger spiritual forces that are wont to affect at the same time or almost at the same time groups of people that have reached a like stage of development. The modern emergence of the free personality from the merely political individual—the voter who in his day succeeded the tribesman and the slave—accounts for the change in the passions and the forms of poetry in Goethe and in Shelley, in Whitman and Henley, in Richard Dehmel and in Henri de Régnier. Thus, too, it is interesting rather than important when M. Kahn says: "I am persuaded and certain, as far as I am concerned, that the influence of music led us to the perception of a poetic form at once more fluid and precise, and that the musical sensations of our youth (not only Wagner, but Beethoven and Schubert) had their influence upon my conception of verse when I was capable of uttering a personal song." "A personal song"— that ambition is the secret of the age and the movement. "The poet shall obey his personal rhythm," M. Vielé-Griffin repeats. "The poet's only guide is rhythm; not a rhythm that has been learned, that is crippled by a thousand rules which others have invented, but a personal rhythm that he must find within himself." Thus M. Adolph Retté summed up the matter so early as 1893 in the *Mercure de France*. Thus only, one may add, did these poets hope to achieve that "personal art" which, according to Gourmont, "is the only art."

In the works of the earliest practitioners of free verse, gifted poets as they all are, the new form had, at times, a *timbre* that was merely quaint or an air of conscious violence. The personal rhythm, especially in the structure of the stanza—or, rather, verse-paragraph—was apt, in the days of protest and polemic, to be more personal than rhythmic. In the hands of those members of the school, however, who were capable of a notable inner development, the new *vers libre* became an instrument of poetic expression that gave not only a new freedom but an ampler and more spiritual music to French verse: an instrument at once plangent and sonorous, capable of both subtle grace and large majesty. It has survived the reactions and new experiments to be chronicled later; it is used by so recent a poet as M. Fernand Gregh as the vehicle of what is, perhaps, his most admirable single poem *Je vis*. . . . :

"Mais à mon tour j'aurai connu le goût chaud de la vie:
J'aurai miré dans ma prunelle,
Petite minute éblouie,

La grande lumière éternelle:
Mais j'aurai bonne joie au grand festin sacré;
Que voudrais-je de plus?
J'aurai vécu . . .
Et je mourrai." [1]

That has neither the stormy power of Verhaeren's *La Foule* nor the noble melancholy of Régnier's *Le Vase*. But any one sensitive to the music of the language in which it is written must feel its native and unforced beauty, the liquid pathos of its lingering cadences.

[1] "But in my turn I shall have known the warm taste of life: I shall have mirrored in my eye-ball, a brief and dazzling minute, the great eternal light; but I shall have a goodly joy in the great, sacred feast; what more would I have wished? I shall have lived . . . And I shall die."

III

THE TRIUMPH OF SYMBOLISM

"La nature paraît sculpter
Un visage nouveau à son éternité;
Tout bouge—et l'on dirait les horizons en marche."

ÉMILE VERHAEREN

" . . . Elle me dit; Sculpte la pierre
Selon la forme de mon corps en tes pensées,
Et fais sourire au bloc ma face claire . . . "

HENRI DE RÉGNIER

THE movement was founded; the instrument of expression was forged. There arose from it two poets of high and memorable character, the two I have already named: Émile Verhaeren (1855–1915) and Henri de Régnier (b. 1864). Though M. Verhaeren died but, as it were, the other day, and M. de Régnier is just arriving at the ripest period of his own genius, there can be no reasonable doubt that these two, at least, of the French

[28]

poets who started as Symbolists have permanently enriched the literature of the world.

They resemble each other in nothing but in the language they use and in certain new liberties of external form. As men and as artists they are deeply divided. Verhaeren is a man of the North, of wild cries and mystic raptures, of boundless exaltations and agonies. There is a touch of fever in his visions both of his Flemish country-side and of the turbulent modern cities that he loved. He sought finally to release his tortured soul from the bondage of self by sinking it, merging it—not like the Germanic mystics of old in God or nature, but in that vast brotherhood of pain and effort that bears the burden and the heat of an industrial civilisation. He was, as M. Léon Balzalgette, one of his most intelligent biographers, says, "a barbarian whom fate doomed to paint his visions by the help of a language made rather to translate the delicate and refined sensations of extreme civilisation." He had no sense of "measure," "tradition," "good taste." He is "with his poetical powers a man of the North, just as truly as Carlyle. . . . " That is well and tellingly put.

From Verhaeren's work there arises finally the vision of a universe in tumult, not wholly free from chaos, midway between formlessness and form; against a black and desolate background flare the silver visions of the soul and the scarlet fires of steel furnaces. In this universe the poet wanders seeking rest, union, finding it at last in an act of complete acceptance, of utter oneness with the forces that shape the world. . . .

His style is, necessarily, wholly alien to the tradition of the Latins. There is a constant straining to express the inexpressible vastness of vision and passion, to put into speech that which transcends it. Thus, almost throughout his work, there is an abundance, sometimes too great an abundance, of strong words. Things are to him "enormous," "formidable," "mad," "anguished," "brutal," ferocious," "bitter," "fevered." The titles of some of his books are instructive in this respect: *The Black Torches (Les Flambeaux noirs)*, *The Hallucinated Country Sides (Les Campagnes halucinées)*, *The Tumultuous Forces (Les Forces tumultueuses)*, *The Multple Splendor (La Multiple Splendeur)*. Everywhere one shares his own impassioned sense of the inadequacy of language, of the weakness of imagery which he strives to overcome by the use of sharp contrasts and of direct and forceful verbs:

"Visages d'encre et d'or trouant l'ombre et la brume." [1]

In other words, one never loses sight of Verhaeren's racial kinship. He is a Fleming, a descendant of the men whom Rembrandt painted —a full-bodied, insatiable, Germanic folk. He was profoundly conscious of this fact and gloried in it:

"Je suis le fils de cette race,
Dont les cerveaux plus que les dents
Sont solides et sont ardents
Et sont voraces.
Je suis le fils de cette race
Ténace,
Qui veut, apres avoir voulu
Encore, encore et encore plus!" [2]

One feels in such verses almost the march and accent of Germanic versification. And Verhaeren

---

[1] "Faces of ink and gold boring the shade and fog."

[2] "I am a son of that race whose brains, more than their teeth, are solid and are ardent and voracious. I am a son of that tenacious race that desires, after having desired the more, more yet and ever more!"

raises this impulse of his blood and race into a philosophic vision and a principle of conduct:

"Et je criais: La force est sainte.
Il faut que l'homme imprime son empreinte
Violemment, sur ses desseins hardis;
Elle est celle qui tient les clefs des paradis
Et dont le large poing en fait tourner les portes." [1]

It is evident that the style and rhythm of such a poet will not seek, first of all, after beauty but after power, that in its failure it will touch violence, in its success sublimity. And that is literally true of Verhaeren's style.

The development of his mind and art is important not only for the student of his verse. Its nature is such that he becomes, by virtue of it, almost symbolical of the pain and hope of his age. In his early volumes *(Les Flammandes, Les Moines)*, he works evidently in the tradition of Rubens: he sets down a large, strong vision of large, strong things. Only in that vision there is already, despite all health and vigor, a deepening

[1] "And I cried out: 'Force itself is sacred. Man must violently stamp his imprint upon his bold designs: it is force that holds the keys of all paradises and whose large hand makes their gates swing open.'"

melancholy, a mystical and subjective gloom. There followed a period of acute mental and physical distress (1887–1890), bordering at times upon the pathological, in which he exalts pain itself with an almost savage note. Gradually he recovered. Love helped him and gentle memories and, at times, exquisite visions such as that of Saint George, the symbol to him of spiritual valor:

> "J'ai mis, en sa pâle main fière,
> Les fleurs tristes de ma douleur." [1]

But the liberating experience, since he could find peace in no form of personal idealism, religious or philosophic, came to him about 1892 through his identification with the Socialist movement. It meant far more to him than a humanitarian hope, though it was that, too: it meant now the possibility of accepting the modern world in its entirety, identifying himself with it, casting off the burden of self. In that inner urgency lay, of course, his weakness. But the process, too, clarified his thinking magnificently and freed him from many of the common and futile causes of moral pain:

---

[1] "'I laid into his proud, pale hand the sad flowers of my pain.'"

"Les droits et les devoirs ? Rêves divers que fait
Devant chaque espoir neuf, la jeunesse du monde !" [1]

He now established in his visions and his verse that contrast between the past and future of civilisation, symbolised for him by the country and the city and the latter's encroachment on the former:

"L'esprit de campagnes était l'esprit de Dieu . . .
L'usine rouge éclat où seuls brillaient les champs,
La fumée à flots noirs rase les toits d'église." [2]

Again and again, as in the turbidly yet greatly imaginative *Les Cordiers*, he compares the long ago with the burning present:

"Jadis—c'était la vie ardente, évocatoire;
La Croix blanche de ciel, la Croix rouge d'enfer
Marchaient, à la clarté des armures de fer,
Chacune à travers sang, vers son ciel de victoire . . .

Voici—c'est une usine; et la matière intense
Et rouge y roule et vibre, en des caveaux,
Où se forgent d'ahan les miracles nouveaux
Qui absorbent la nuit, le temps et le distance." [3]

[1] "Rights and duties? They are varied dreams that the world's youth dreams in the face of each new hope."
[2] "The spirit of the country-sides was the spirit of God. . . . The factory flares where once the lonely fields shone; the smoke in black waves grazes the roofs of the church."
[3] "Once on a time—life was all ardor and full of visions: The

But he drew his profoundest inspiration from the crowd *(La Foule)* of great cities. Here, in this universal, laboring heart he found the meaning of life, the hope for the future, liberation for his own soul. In these cities and crowds, he cried:

> "Je sens grandir et s'exalter en moi
> Et fermenter, soudain, mon coeur multiplié." [1]

He saw the cities with all the accustomed fevered ardor of his vision. But in them he found his ultimate hope:

> "Un vaste espoir, venu de l'inconnu déplace
> L'équilibre ancien dont les âmes sont lasses." [2]

And not only hope, it must be repeated, but freedom. For he found here that "great hour in which the aspects of the world change, wherein that seems strange which once was just and holy,

white Cross of heaven, the red Cross of hell marched, in the shining of iron armor, each across blood, toward its victorious sky. . . ." "To-day—yonder is a factory; matter, intense and red, rolls and vibrates there in the vaults wherein are forged with bitter labor those new miracles that swallow night and time and distance."

[1] I feel my multiplied heart suddenly grow great and seethe and exalt itself within me.

[2] "A vast hope arisen from the unknown displaces the ancient equilibrium of which men's souls are weary."

wherein man ascends towards the summits of another faith, where madness itself, in the storms, forges a new truth!"   With this blind communal birth of new truth and new law he strove to be at one:

> "Engouffre-toi,
> Mon coeur, en ces foules . . ." [1]

His passion and his vision grew in apocalyptic fervor on this note.   He alone among the greater modern poets dedicated himself utterly to the extremest form of democratic faith—faith in the prophetic and creative power of the mere mass:

> "Mets en accord ta forces avec les destinées
> Que la foule, sans le savoir
> Promulgue, en cette nuit d'angoisse illuminée.
> Ce que sera demain, le droit et le devoir,
> Seule, elle en a l'instinct profond,
> Et l'univers total s'attelle et collabore
> Avec ses milliers de causes qu'on ignore
> A chaque effort vers le futur, qu'elle élabore,
> Rouge et tragique, à l'horizon." [2]

[1] "Engulf thyself, my heart, in these crowds . . ."
[2] "Place thy strength in harmony with those destinies which, without knowing it, the crowd promulgates in this night lit by agonies. Of what the morrow will bring forth of right and duty the crowd alone has the deep instinct. And the whole uni-

That is very fervent and very noble writing.   Yet
one feels, I think, throughout such passages, a sense
not of the highest strength—nothing of quiet
power.   He fled from his too troubled and in-
sistent self to this extreme faith because he could
not clarify that self or calm it; because he failed
to be, in the deeper and serener sense, the master
of his soul.   A man and a poet almost but never
wholly great. . . .

To pass from Verhaeren to Régnier is to recall,
involuntarily, Taine's old theory of the effect of
climate on literature.   For can any one be, more
than Verhaeren, the creature of a fog-bound coast,
a storm-beaten plain, a group of rain-swept cities?
And then that golden-winged Muse *(La Muse aux
ailes d'or)* of Henri de Régnier—does she not
move in luminous gardens under a temperate but
radiant sky, does she not hear the murmur of clear
waters on the wooded slopes, does she not sing her
austere dream of beauty in a calm and starry evenfall . . . ?   No one could be more Latin than

verse puts itself in harness and with its thousand causes of
which we know nothing labors at each effort toward the future
which the mass draws broadly, red and tragic, upon the horizon."

[37]

Régnier.   Modern as he is, exquisite practitioner of free verse, mystical lover of beauty, he has the " divine elegance" of Vergil, the lovely *suavitas*, the discreet but piercing melancholy.   He attains these qualities, of course, at the price of large and definite exclusions.   The harsh cries, the tragic questions of the modern world, never break in upon the walled garden of his imaginings.   He lives, as M. Jean de Gourmont has said, "in royal land-scapes, palaces of gold and marble which are noth-ing in reality but the setting in which the poet has chosen to place his dream."   I would not have him otherwise.   The world sets our hearts and brains on fire.   Here, in the poetry of Régnier, is a place of ease and rest and noble solitude like that "great, good place" in Henry James' story, here beauty, though with so new a grace, goes through her eternal gesture and lays her hand upon the fever of our eyes.   I would have him always in that attitude of his *Discours en Face de la Nuit:*

"Je parlerai, debout et du fond de mon songe. . . . " [1]

[1] "I shall speak standing erect and from the depth of my dream."

And I would have his liquid voice die on the ear

"Avec l'aube qui rit aux larmes des fontaines,
Avec le soir qui pleure aux rires des ruisseaux." [1]

His style is unique, both in its diction and its imagery, for an extraordinary blending of modern sensitiveness with classic clearness and frugality. Constantly, after his earliest symbolist poems, he employs the traditional Hellenic myths and legends to body forth his vision; he does so even in the freest of modern verse and so adds to those myths and legends a new freshness and a more troubling grace. The Latin in him is unconquerable, the immemorial tradition absorbed him, until quite recently, more and more. As early as 1896 he wrote lines which would startle no one if found on some page of the Greek Anthology or of Tibullus. There is the same frugal restraint in sadness and in beauty.

"Et mes yeux qui t'ont vu sont las d'avoir pleuré
L'inexorable absence où tu t'es retiré
Loin de mes bras pieux et de ma bouche triste . . ." [2]

[1] "With dawn that laughs with the tears of the fountains, with evening that weeps to the laughter of the rivulets."
[2] "And my eyes which have seen thee are weary of having

One recalls, I think, those other verses—as tender and as full of longing—of the Roman elegist:

"Te spectem suprema mihi cum venerit hora,
Te teneam moriens deficiente manu." [1]

His growing preoccupation with beauty in its antique forms may be studied in the admirable titles of his later volumes: *Games Rustic and Divine (Les Jeux rustiques et divins), The Medals of Clay (Les Medailles d'Argile), The Winged Sandal (La Sandale ailée.)* It would be doing him a grave wrong, however, to imagine that he takes up again any Neo-classic tradition; his inspiration and its sources are as alien as possible to either the method of the Renaissance or of the Seventeenth Century. He has chosen the imagery of the ancients because he has seen and felt it anew, for himself, and has deliberately used it in that vibrant, ultra-modern verse of his:

"Un jour, encor,
Entre les feuilles d'ocre et d'or

wept over the inexorable absence to which thou hast withdrawn, far from my pious arms and my sad mouth."

[1] "May I see thee when my supreme hour shall have come, may I, dying, hold thee with my failing hand."

Du bois, je vis, avec ses jambes de poil jaune,
Danser un faune." [1]

He finds the timelessness of beauty best interpreted thus. "For Poetry," he writes, "has neither yesterday nor to-morrow, nor to-day. It is the same everywhere. What it desires is to see itself beautiful and is indifferent, if only its beauty be reflected, whether the glass is the natural spring of the forest or some mirror in which a subtle artifice shows unto it its divine countenance in the crystal limpidness of a fictive and imaginary water." One may assent to that theory or one may not. It is by the light of such thought, at all events, that M. de Régnier has written the most beautiful French verses of his age.

He does not, of course, deny his modernity, his origin in time. He was a pupil of Verlaine and heard Mallarmé in his youth and wrote:

"Il neige dans mon coeur des souffrances cachées. . . ." [2]

with its obvious reminiscence of Verlaine's famous:

[1] "Again, one day, amid the forest's leaves of ochre and of gold I saw a faun dance with his yellow haired legs."
[2] "It snows in my heart with hidden sufferings . . ."

> "Il pleure dans mon coeur
> Comme il pleut sur la ville. . . ." [1]

He wrote:

> "O mon âme, le soir est triste sur hier. . . ." [2]

And he proclaimed in those years:

> "La Terre douloureuse a bu le sang des Rêves. . . ." [3]

And his versification is as wavering and as untraditional in his last volume as in his first. The truth is that he took refuge in the antique vision of beauty from the excessive sensitiveness of his own temper, from the over-delicacy of his own pride. Life had too great a power to wound him and so he turned, in poetry, to those objects of contemplation and those images that have no pang but the pang of beauty:

> "Car la forme, l'odeur et la beauté des choses
> Sont le seul souvenir dont on ne souffre pas." [4]

[1] "It weeps in my heart as it rains on the town . . ."
[2] "O my soul, the evening is sad over yesterday . . ."
[3] "The anguished earth has drunk the blood of dreams."
[4] "For the form, the fragrance and the beauty of things are the only memory from which one does not suffer."

In his last volume there is directer and more naked speech as in the powerful passion of *Le Reproche*, the grave and elevated frankness of *L'Accueil*, the remarkable avowal of *La Forêt*. And he may continue upon this path. The marvellous beauty of the work of his middle years, however, will remain in its union of classic grace and modern subtlety.

That union was founded upon a personal interpretation of the post-Kantian idealism which came to France in the early days of the Symbolist movement. "I have feigned," says M. de Régnier, "that gods have spoken with me. . . . " "Listen: there is someone behind the echo, erect amid the universal life who bears the double arch and the double torch and who is divinely identical with us." That spirit of universal beauty who is at one with the All and at one with us arises out of that divine union in an hundred shadows of himself and these shadows of the "invisible Face" the poet has sought to grave upon medals "soft and silvery as the pale dawn, of gold as ardent as the sun, of brass as sombre as the night—of every metal that sounds clear as joy or deep as glory or love or death." And he has made the loveliest "of lovely clay, fragile and dry." And men have come to him and smiled and counted the medals and said: "He is skilful," and have passed on smiling:

"Aucun de vous n'a donc vu
Que mes mains tremblaient de tendresse,
Que tout le grand songe terrestre
Vivait en moi pour vivre en eux
Que je gravais aux métaux pieux
Mes Dieux,
Et qu'ils étaient le visage vivant
De ce que nous avons senti des roses,
De l'eau, du vent,
De la forêt et de la mer,
De toutes choses
En notre chair
Et qu'ils sont nous divinement." [1]

That passage completes the statement of the philosophical background of Régnier's poetry. It

[1] "Did not but one of you then see that my hands trembled with tenderness, that all the great terrestrial dream lived in me to live again in them whom I engraved on pious metals—those gods of mine,—and that they were the living countenance of all that we have felt of roses, of water and the wind, of the forest and the sea, of all things in our flesh, and that, in some divine way, they are ourselves."

may also serve to illustrate the flexibility, the expressiveness and range of his free verse music, even though it has not the ampler cadences of *Le Vase*. But indeed, M. de Régnier's versification is always —at least to a foreigner's ear—mere perfection. His music is usually grave and slow and deep, rarely very energetic, but of a sweetness that never cloys. He has used rime and assonance, he has denied himself no measure of freedom and variety, but he has also taken the alexandrine and drawn from it a note of profound spiritual grace and a more inner music.

It is difficult to choose among the other poets who proceeded from Symbolism. They are many and there is hardly one of them who has not written memorably at times. But this is not a history of the modern poetry of France and it will suffice to speak briefly of Jean Moréas, of MM. Francis Vielé-Griffin and Stuart Merrill, of the late Albert Samain and Rémy de Gourmont and, still more briefly, of those younger men who carry the symbolist inspiration and method into the immediate present.

Jean Moréas (1856–1910) a notably gifted and flexible Greek threw himself early and ardently into the Symbolist movement. But, by 1891, in his *Le Pèlerin Passioné*, he attempted to create a diversion, to found a new school, the briefly famous *École romane*. He was concerned largely with the question of poetic diction and, through it, of poetic vision. He desired to bring about a "communion of the French Middle Ages and Renaissance with the principle of the modern soul," by using a selection from the archaic words of the *Pléiade* and even of the *Roman de la Rose*. Hence M. Anatole France promptly called him the Ronsard of Symbolism. And the lyrics of the *Pèlerin passioné* have, no doubt, a certain old-world sweetness wherever the obvious archaisms do not give them a somewhat obscure and artificial grace. His earlier symbolist verse, in which he took some very quaint and charming liberties of versification and poetic manner—

("Parmi les marroniers, parmi les
Lilas blancs, les lilas violets. . . . ") [1]

[1] "Among the chestnut trees, among the white lilacs, the violet lilacs . . ."

—are of the stuff of dreams and have a dreamy cadence:

"Voix qui revenez, bercez-nous, berceuses voix. . . ." [1]

Finally he left behind him both Symbolism and
his own *École romane*. "These things concern
me no longer," he confessed in his middle age and,
withdrawing into solitude, he wrote his last work:
Les Stances (1901-1905). In these poems he
returns to the traditional verse, to the traditional
stanzaic forms. They have an extraordinary pu-
rity of poetic outline, a notable dignity of speech
and imagination, a just and proud perfection. It
was the Hellenic soul in him, one must suppose,
that made his last work so memorable an example
of the classical spirit in modern poetry. His
changes of mood and manner and theory were not
without their influence upon the younger poets and
no less a man that M. Paul Fort has written:

"Ce que je dois a Moréas ne peut être dit en paroles." [2]

The American, M. Francis Vielé-Griffin (b.
1864) was one of the very active founders of the

[1] "O voices that return, cradle us, cradling voices . . ."
[2] "What I owe to Moréas cannot be expressed in words."

Symbolist school and has remained true to it ever since. A poet of rare lyrical gift, he has always been concerned with his "interior vision" and has continued to hold that "conviction, common to Shelley, Wagner and Mallarmé, that reality is a creation of the soul and art a superimposed creation." With him, as with so many of the poets of modern France—Jewish, Greek, Flemish, Anglo-Saxon, Alemanic Swiss—one is tempted, wrongly perhaps, to attribute certain qualities of thought and style to racial origin. It is a fact, at all events, that M. Vielé-Griffin is often hauntingly lyrical in a sense that is not characteristically Latin and that in his mingling of verses of seven and eight syllables one seems to detect the introduction of an English cadence:

> "N'est-il une chose au Monde,
> Chère, à la face du ciel
> —Un rire, un rêve, une ronde,
> Un rayon d'aurore ou de miel. . . . "[1]

He is a poet who rarely touches the imagination without also touching the heart, whose music

[1] "Is there a thing in the world, dear, in the face of the sky— a laugh, a dream, a song, a beam of the dawn or of honey."

ranges from a lyrical lift to the fullness and grave-
ness of the elegy.

The other American who has become a modern
French poet is M. Stuart Merrill (b. 1868). His
general character as a man and an artist is at once
evident from a correct interpretation of his own
words: "Modern society is a badly written poem
which one must be active in correcting. A poet,
in the etymological sense, remains a poet everywhere and it is his duty to bring back some loveliness upon the earth." Accordingly, M. Merrill,
a revolutionary Socialist, has given unstintingly
both of himself and of his fortune to his chosen
cause. In art, on the other hand, he has been pre-
occupied with beauty alone. His poems are
woven upon the loom of dreams; they have a
visionary magnificence, a glint as of shadows upon
gold. Once at least in *Les Poings à la Porte* he
has come near sublimity. His music has often a
slow and lingering quality and he has used, with
notable success, lines—so rare in French—that are
longer than the alexandrine:

"L'Amour entrera toujours comme un ami dans notre
   maison,

T'ai-je répondu, écoutant le bruit des feuilles qui tom-
bent." [1]

In turning to Albert Samain (1858–1900) we
come once more upon the unmistakably Latin temperament. The first of his two celebrated volumes *Au Jardin de L'Infante* (1893) is purely
symbolist in inspiration and quality; in the
second *Aux Flancs du Vase* (1898) he turns again
to the beauty of the visible world, of the immortal gesture held fast as in the plastic arts which is,
after all, perhaps the most characteristic method
of French poetry. His verse here is still free and
flowing and trembling; the pictures are sculptured
or painted, and poetry adds nothing to this art
except the element of motion before the final and
memorable gesture is achieved. All his best
poems follow this method and so he attains the
white, sculptural beauty of *Xanthis*, the ruddy,
flame-like glow of *Pannyre aux Talons d'Or*
(XXXVI).

The chief quality of the late M. Rémy de Gourmont's (1858–1915) character was an extreme

---

[1] "Love will enter always like a friend into our house, I an-
swered thee while listening to the noise of leaves that fall."

subtlety—subtlety of mind and subtlety of the senses. The first made him a critic of the highest order even in a country of great critics. He carried far beyond Jules Lemaître what is rather foolishly known as the impressionist method in criticism: the plain and sensible belief, namely, that a work of art is precious not through the tribal or social elements in it, but through the personal, that art knows no ought-ness of convention or precedent and that the test of beauty, different in that respect from truth, is a pragmatic one. . . . His poetry, of which he did not write a great deal, addresses itself to the nerves, to the finer senses. It is keen and strange and pale and, at its best, of a very individual music though always adhering to the prosody of the Symbolists.

The younger members of the school, the late Charles Guérin (1873–1907), M. Camille Mauclair (who is also a critic of distinction), M. Henry Bataille (the well-known playwright), M. Henri Barbusse (who recently achieved international fame with *Le Feu*), M. Henri Spiess and M. Fernand Gregh, have all continued the now familiar methods of modern French poetry. Each has contributed his personal vision and his personal note. But he has contributed these to a kind of poetry now firmly established and well recognisable: poetry that lives in the dawn and dusk of the mind, that sees its visions in the state of revery and projects its own shadows upon the face of the world—whose voice is a wavering music, the notes of a flute upon the breeze. . . .

IV

"Il dit je ne sais quoi de triste, bon et pur."
FRANCIS JAMMES

"La terre est le soleil en moi sont en cadence,
et toute la nature est entrée dans mon cœur."
PAUL FORT

THERE has been no reaction against Symbolism in France. I am not at all sure that the very youngest group, with some exaggerations in prosodic matters, has not merely returned to the essential taste and method of the early eighteen hundred and nineties. In the meantime, however, there have appeared two powerful talents who, a rare thing in France, stand aside and alone, members of no group, no school, no *cénacle:* MM. Francis Jammes (b. 1868) and Paul Fort (b. 1872).

Charles Guérin, in a set of very pure and very touching verses addressed to M. Jammes calls that poet a "son of Vergil." The saying has been repeated because M. Jammes, unlike the average French man of letters, lives in the country (at Orthez in the Hautes-Pyrénées) and writes about country matters which he understands admirably. Thus he recalls, in a superficial way, the poet of the *Georgics*. But one quotation, and a hackneyed one, from those magnificent poems and one brief confession from M. Jammes will show the absurdity of the comparison and also define the French poet's character. Everyone knows the Vergilian lines:

"Felix qui potuit rerum cognoscere causas. . . ." [1]

M. Jammes prefaced his first collection of poems with these words: "My God, you have called me among men. Here I am. I suffer and I love. I have spoken with the voice which you have given me. I have written with the words which you taught my father and my mother who transmitted them to me. I pass along the road like a burdened ass at whom children laugh and who droops his

[1] "Happy he who has been able to understand the causes of things."

head. I shall go when you would have me, whither you would have me go. . . . The angelus rings." There is nothing here of the sad intellectual valor of the Augustans. It is the note of Saint Francis, the humble brother of the birds and beasts. . . . In a word, M. Jammes is a Catholic. So wholly a Catholic that one need not speak of intellectual submission in his case. He was born with the light of faith as his only guide and sees life with the wide-eyed reverential wonder of a little child or a great saint. He has the child's and the saint's simple-hearted familiarity with divine things:

"Ce n'est pas vous, mon Dieu,
qui, sur les joues en roses, posez la mort bleue." [1]

and the tender and vivid sense of the human elements in his divinities:

"Rappelez-vous, mon Dieu, devant l'enfant qui meurt,
que vous vivez toujours auprès de votre Mère." [2]

So, too, as an artist, he is like the nameless sculp-

[1] "It is not you, my God, who on the rosy cheeks will lay the blue of death."
[2] "Recall, my God, before the dying child, that you live always near your own mother."

tors who adorned the Mediæval cathedrals, an humble craftsman in the light of God's glory, desiring nothing for himself:

"Et, comme un adroit ouvrier
tient sa truelle alourdie de mortier,
je veux, d'un coup, á chaque fois porter
du bon ouvrage au mur de ma chaumière." [1]

He is aware, of course, of the life of his own age. He has read, as he says, "novels and verses made in Paris by men of talent." But these men and their works seem very forlorn and sad to him. He would have them come to his own country-side; for it is in the stillness of the fields and farms that the peace of God is to be found:

"Alors ils souriront en fumant dans leur pipe,
et, s'ils souffrent encore, car les hommes sont tristes,
ils guériront beaucoup en écoutant les cris
des éperviers pointus sur quelque métairie." [2]

His own happiness is untroubled, his own submission to the divine will complete. Like Saint

[1] "And as a skilful workman holds his trowel, heavy with mortar, I would, at once, each time add some goodly work to the wall of my cottage."

[2] "Then they will smile while smoking their pipes, and, if they suffer still, for men are sad, they will be greatly cured by hearing the cries of the slim sparrow-hawks over the farmlands."

Francis he has grasped the uttermost meaning of the Christian virtue of humility and prays to pass into Paradise with the asses:

"... et faites que, penché dans ce séjour des âmes
sur vos divines eaux, je sois pareil aux âns
qui mireront leur humble et douce pauvreté
à la limpidité de l'amour éternel." [1]

These quotations, fragmentary and brief as they are, will already have made clear some of the qualities of this extraordinary poet. The saint-like simplicity of his vision has really, on the purely descriptive side, made him a naturalist. For he is no burning mystic, no St. John of the Cross or Richard Crashaw, but a humble child of the Church who sees the immediate things of this world very soberly and clearly as they appear in their objective nature:

"Il y a aussi le chien malade
regardant tristement, couché dans les salades
venir la grande mort qu'il ne comprendra pas." [2]

[1] "Leaning over your divine waters in that sojourning place of souls, cause me to be like to the asses who will mirror their humble and gentle poverty in the limpidity of the eternal love."
[2] "There is also the sick dog sadly watching, where he lies amid the lettuce, great death approach which he will not understand."

But he is always conscious of the relations which these things, according to his faith, sustain to the divine. And so, when his own dog dies, he exclaims:

"Ah! faites, mon Dieu, si vous me donnez la grâce
de Vous voir face à Face aux jours d'Éternité,
faites qu'un pauvre chien contemple face à face
celui qui fut son dieu parmi l'humanité." [1]

As becomes his spiritual character, M. Jammes has discarded all the vain pomp and splendor of verse, even the subtler and quieter graces of the Symbolists. His tone is conversational, almost casual; his sentences have the structure of prose. He uses rime or assonance or suddenly fails to rime at all. He seems merely bent on telling the simple and beautiful things in his heart as quietly as possible. What constitutes his eminence, his very high eminence, as an artist is the fact that his prosaic simplicity of manner, his naïve matter-of-factness, his apparently (but only apparently) slovenly technique are so used as to make for a

[1] "Ah, my God, if you grant me the grace of seeing you face to face in the days of Eternity, then let a poor dog contemplate face to face him who was his god among men."

new style in French poetry—a naturalistic style that rises constantly to a high and noble elevation of speech, and rises to that elevation, as Wordsworth sought to do, by using the simplest words in the simplest order. Briefly, he does not adorn things until they become poetical; he sees them poetically. His imagination and his heart transform them, not his diction or his figures of speech. Is that not the highest aim of poetry? And yet it were thrusting aside some very elementary and obvious considerations to call M. Jammes a great poet. A great artist he is—but not a great poet. For, except on the purely pictorial side, his subject matter, the intellectual content of his work is, necessarily, without significance or permanent validity. It has subjective truth only. So, it may be said, has the substance of most modern verse. True! But a subjectivity that finds harmonious echoes in a thousand souls achieves, after all, the only kind of objectivity, of reality that we know. That kind of reality and therefore significance M. Jammes, as a Catholic in the twentieth century, has largely denied himself. To his fellow-villagers at Orthez, who share his faith, he will seem merely curious as a writer: to the intellectual world of the present and the future he will seem a little curious—however admirably and highly gifted—as a man.

The fame of M. Paul Fort has attached, so far, mainly to the new kind of writing which he is said to have invented. He himself has protested against this, and it is but natural that he should. It is equally natural for the public to fix its attention upon the startling innovations of which he is the author. But I must hasten to add that the revolutionary character of these innovations has been greatly exaggerated. In matters strictly prosodic M. Fort employs, as a rule, a principle which is conservative enough in its nature. And yet his style of writing is new, and not only new but charmingly successful and he himself one of the most remarkable and delightful poets of our time.

He writes and prints his verse as prose. Instead of stanzas, the eye is given paragraphs, now long, now short. But I must emphasise the fact that the length and rhythmic character of the paragraphs in any given poem is, nearly always, the same. Thus the one essential characteristic of verse (in the narrower sense), the recurrence of rhythm-groups that are felt to be equal in time, is preserved. If now one begins to analyse these paragraphs it will be found that, with definite but not very numerous exceptions, they resolve themselves into lesser equal rhythm-groups or—lines. And these lines are, granting many exceptions again, verses of eight, ten or twelve syllables. Here is an example of two octosyllabic verses printed as prose:

"Pourquoi renouer l'amourette? C'est-y bien la peine d'aimer?" [1]

And here of two deccasyllabic verses:

"Ah! que de joie, la flûte et la musette troublent nos cœurs de leurs accords charmants. . . ." [2]

It is in the use of the twelve-syllabled verse, of the alexandrine, that M. Fort is most original. The rhythmic unit that he uses is in reality the

[1] "Why knot again our broken love? Is the sorrow of love worth while?"

[2] "Ah, what delight, the flute and the bagpipe trouble our hearts with their charming harmonies . . ."

hemistich or stave of six syllables without, however, letting the full movement of the alexandrine
ever escape the ear entirely. Thus he can constantly use internal rime or assonance and also un-
rimed end syllables. To illustrate this manner
of his fully I shall quote a rather long verse-paragraph, italicising the syllables that have assonance
or rime. And I use a paragraph in which M. Fort,
who is rather irresponsible in this respect, allows
their full, traditional value to all the mute *e*'s but
two:

"O grave, austère pluie, où monte l'âme des pi*erres* et
qui portez en vous une froide lumi*ère*, glacez mon âme en
f*eu*, rendez mon cœur sév*ère*, imposez la fraîch*eur* aux
mains que je vous *tends!* L'averse tombe un p*eu* . . .
elle tombe . . . j'at*tends* . . . Quoi! la lune se lève?
Quoi! l'orage est pas*sé?* Quoi! tout le ciel en fl*eurs?* et
l'air sent, par bouf*fées*, l'oeillet, la tubér*euse*, la rose et
la poussi*ère?* Une étoile d'amour sur le Louvre a glis*sé?*
J'achète des bouqu*ets!* quoi! je suis insen*sé?* Et je ris
de mon cœur, et je cours chez Man*on*, des roses plein les
bras, implorer mon pard*on?*" [1]

[1] "O grave, austere rain into which has risen the soul of
jewels and who carry in yourself a cold light, frost over
my soul on fire, make my heart severe, lay freshness on
the hands that I stretch out to you! The shower falls for a
little . . . it falls . . . I wait . . . What! does the moon arise?

[62]

This exceedingly beautiful paragraph, closely studied, will be seen to consist in reality of twelve alexandrine verses. But the middle cæsura is so sharp that the individual music of the hemistich is constantly stressed. Of these twelve alexandrines the first, second and third rime (though not quite purely, perhaps), the fourth and fifth, the sixth and seventh. The eighth is blank though I am rather sure that M. Fort means us to feel *poussière* as echoing the earlier *sevère* and *lumière;* the ninth rimes with both the first and second hemistich of the tenth, a device which accelerates the movement of the verse, and the eleventh and twelfth rime again quite regularly. In addition there is, I am equally sure, a not wholly unconscious element of assonance in the stave endings: *feu, fraîcheur, peu, fleurs, tubéreuse.*

If this verse-paragraph be accepted as fairly representative of M. Fort's manner of writing, and if my analysis of it be correct, it is obviously

What! has the storm gone by? What? Does the sky burst into flowers? and the air smells, by gusts, of the carnation and the tuberose, of roses and of dust? Has a star of love glided over the Louvre? I buy posies! How! am I beside myself? And I laugh from my heart, and I run to Manon, my arms full of roses, to implore my forgiveness?"

wrong to regard him as primarily a writer of very free verse or of mere poetic prose with an occasional rime. And so the question arises: Is his typographical form a mere crotchet? It is not. One need but read once more the paragraph I have quoted—read it quite naturally and simply now without any thought of its prosodic method—to feel that here is a new poetic style in French, incomparable in its ease, its grace, its fluidity, following and never doing violence to the emotion, modulated to the very tones of the human voice. Or, more specifically, M. Fort's manner of writing and printing gives him these advantages: The sentences are not broken by prosodic divisions but flow on freely. Yet the verse music is never lost. The diction can be as natural, as unpoetical (in the older sense) as he pleases. Yet it is never felt to jar through its contrast with the associations of traditional verse. He can restrict or multiply his rimes at will and unobtrusively and hence use them to express the color and tone of the immediate poetic mood and moment. So he achieves, I must use the words once more, an ease,

[64]

a grace, a fluidity of poetic movement which are as new as they are beautiful.

His manner of writing grew naturally from his character as a man and a poet. Whether upon some reasoned philosophic view or not, M. Fort is satisfied with the appearances of things. The beauty, the charm, the quaintness, the light and shade of the visible world—whether in nature or in the gestures of present and historic man or in the colorful and significant events in his own life —these suffice him. He thrills with the beauty and interest, the play and manifoldness of the visible. He keeps himself passive and lets the beauty of the world strike endless music from him. He hesitates to cut and shape and pattern the music of the world's beauty which, like the melody of Wagner, is without pause or end. Long ago, in his earlier *Ballades françaises* he wrote:

"Laisse ordonner le ciel à tes yeux, sans comprendre, et crée de ton silence la musique des nuits." [1]

[1] "Let the sky order (things) for thine eyes, without understanding them, and create with thy silence the music of the nights."

And more recently and directly in the really magnificent *Vision harmonieuse de la Terre* of his *Hymns de Feu:*

"Et ne vous voyez pas que les hommes seraient dieux, s'ils voulaient m'écouter, laisser vivre leurs sens, dans le vent, sur la terre, en plein ciel, et loin d'eux! Ah, que n'y mettent ils un peu de complaisance! Tout l'univers alors (récompense adorable!) serait leur âme éparse, leur cœur inépuisable. Et que dis-je? Ils ont tous le moyen d'être heureux. 'Laisse penser ton sens, homme, et tu es ton Dieu.'" [1]

If there is danger in so complete a surrender to the sensible and the visible, that danger has not touched M. Fort or troubled the health of his soul. He is the serenest and most joyous of modern poets, though he can be deeply grave and tender. His verse has something of the blowing of the winds of spring, of the ripple and flow of the earth's waters. It communicates to us a sense of the undying delight that is in his own heart.

---

[1] "And do you not see that men would be gods, if they would but hear me, would but let their senses live in the wind, upon earth, in the full sky, and far from them? Ah, why do they not strive to yield a little there! All the universe (adorable reward) would be their dispersed soul, their inexhaustible heart. And, what do I say? They all have the means of being happy. 'Let thy senses think for thee, O man, and thou art thy God.'"

Among the slightly older or younger contemporaries of M. Fort various poetic methods and kinds have been cultivated. M. Pierre Louys (b. 1870) may be called a Neo-Parnassien. His work is chiseled and lustrous, but a little conscious and hard. M. Edmond Rostand's (b. 1868) genius shows to less advantage in his personal lyrics and ballads than in the glow and abundance of his famous plays. He is, of course, in the strictly French sense, a Neo-Romantic, a descendant of Lamartine and Hugo. So also is M. Léo Larguier (b. 1878) who clings to the romantic alexandrine, but whose admirable talent persuades the ear as well as the emotions. MM. Paul Souchon (b. 1874) and Maurice Magre (b. 1878) have cultivated an intelligent and agreeable naturalism which one would like to see flourish in the French poetry of to-day more than it does.

I pass on, quite briefly, to the latest movement, the youngest group. The aims of these poets are not yet very clearly defined; their names are scarcely known beyond certain circles in France. One may mention MM. André Spire, Léon Deu-

bel, Réné Arcos, Jules Romains, Charles Vildrac
and Georges Duhamel. Several of them, notably
MM. Spire and Duhamel, are cultivating free
verse not in the symbolist sense but in the contemporary American sense of Miss Amy Lowell
and Mr. Edgar Lee Masters. What effects of
permanent importance or beauty can be thus
achieved in the very fluid medium of French remains to be seen. The longer lines, as in the
third paragraph of M. Duhamel's *Annunciation*
(LIX) tend to approach the alexandrine rhythm;
the shorter lines, as in the last paragraph of the
same poem, seem often about to fall into some
verse pattern dimly present in the poet's mind.
Whether using any such pattern or not, all these
poets have thrown off the last restraints of the
older French prosody and strive after a larger,
subtler, more intellectual music. Their understanding of this whole matter has been set down
very clearly and acutely by MM. Vildrac and Duhamel in their *Notes sur la Technique poétique*
(1910). According to this little treatise a ten-
able theory of versification must be "based upon
the inner (subjective) metric and phonetic rela-

tions." These relations seem to demand, in every verse or line, a constant element or rhythmic unit —either the first or second stave. If both parts or staves of the line conform to this norm, the verse is regular or traditional. If the rhythmic unit be represented but once in each line, if, in other words, each line consist of a rhythmic constant plus a rhythmic variable, the verse is free. Some close observation of modern verse of different types will, I think, convince any competent reader that this theory is far more sensible and helpful than such statements of prosodic principle are apt to be. It is too soon, of course, to offer a definite critical interpretation of these, the youngest poets of France. But one may say that, like the Symbolists, though with even larger liberties of form, they deal with their subjective vision of things, that they, too, have a tendency to withdraw from the dust and heat of the race into the twilit chambers of the soul. . . .

That withdrawal characterises, with exceptions more apparent than real, all the poets of modern France. Verhaeren seems an exception, but we must remember that he was not a Frenchman at all; M. Jammes seems another, but he has withdrawn from the life of thought as truly as the others have from the life of fact. In practically all the modern poetry of France the substance of literature has been transmuted into the stuff of dreams, transposed into the regions of revery. The subjectivity of this poetry is so high that it has absorbed the world into itself. After centuries of a literary life in which the social, the general, the typical, the objective employed all the creative energies of France, these poets could not go beyond the discovery of the world within, the simple finding of their self-hood. But there has been among them hitherto no personality so balanced, so fully self-achieved as to grapple with reality, interpreting or transforming it by the power of the creative intellect, of the creative imagination. That, I take it, should be the next step, the next development in the poetry of France. A movement that brought forth such personalities would give to French literature a poetry more bracing, even though less charming, not quite so beautiful but more valorous and severe.

THE POETS OF MODERN FRANCE

Art only, when all's dust
Through endless years shall dwell,
The bust
Outlasts the citadel.

The austere coin that lies
Beneath a digger's heel
Shall rise
A Cæsar to reveal.

The gods have fled their fanes:
Eternal art alone
Remains—
Stronger than brass or stone.

THÉOPHILE GAUTIER

STÉPHANE MALLARMÉ

I

APPARITION

THE moon grew sad.   The tear-stained seraphim
Adream drew with their bows amid the dim
Mist of calm flowers from failing viol-strings
White grief that to the azure petal clings.—
You had first kissed me on that blessèd day.
My thought in its strange, self-tormenting way
Felt all the subtle melancholy sting
Which, even without regret, the gathering
Of any dream leaves in the dreamer's heart.
Mine eyes fixed on the stones I walked apart
When, with your sunny hair, in that old street
And in the gloom you came with laughter sweet,
Like to that fairy with great aureole
Who once, in dreams of childhood, touched my
        soul,
And who from half-closed hands would ever throw
Clusters of fragrant stars like gleaming snow.

PAUL VERLAINE

II

MY FAMILIAR DREAM

OFTEN a strange and poignant dream is mine
Of an unknown lady whom I love and who
Loves me, forever one yet other, too,
And constant only in her love divine.

Only for her my heart's confusions shine,
Only for her, alas, who can gaze through
My enigmatic soul, who heals the dew
On my pale forehead with her tears benign.

Is she dark, russet, blonde? Her name! Who
    knows?
Sweet and sonorous as the name of those
Beloved ones whom life to exile drove.

Her eyes are with a marble calmness filled,
And her grave voice holds the faint echo of
The cadence of dear voices that are stilled.

III

In the old park, lonely and bound by frost
Two forms just passed and were in darkness lost.

Their lips are pale and moist, their eyes are dead,
Almost inaudible the words they said.

In the old park, lonely and bound by frost,
Two ghosts recalled the perished days they lost.

"Do you remember our old, mad delight?"
"Why would you have me think of it to-night?"

"Still at my name does your heart throb and glow?
And in your dreams your soul still sees me?"—
    "No."

"O goodly days of joy that we have seen
When our lips clung and clung . . ."   "It may
    have been!"

"How blue was heaven and how our hope out-
    spread!"
"To a black sky those perished hopes have fled!"

They walk recalling a wild, graceless day,
And only night can hear the words they say.

IV

SAD and lost I walked where wide
And treacherous the roadways are.
Your dear hand was still my guide.

Pale on the horizon far
A frail hope of day was shed.
Your glance was my morning-star.

No sound but his own echoing tread
Brightened the poor wanderer's thought.
Your voice spoke of hope ahead.

My heart with gloom and terror fraught
Wept at the melancholy sight;
Love the exquisite victor brought

Us to each other in delight.

V

THE keyboard which frail fingers gently stir
Gleams in the rose-grey evening incomplete,
While with a shadowy and wing-like whir
An old tune, very faint and very sweet,
Flutters and falters, timid and discreet,
Here where so long the perfume spoke of her.

Can it be gaiety, can it be pain
That sways and teases my poor heart at it?
What would you have of me, soft, mocking strain?
What did you want, O quavering refrain
That through the open window soon will flit
And in the little garden die again?

VI

Too red, too red the roses were,
Too black the ivy on the tree—

Dear, at the trembling of your hair
All my despair comes back to me.

Too blue and tender was the sky,
The sea too green, the air too sweet—

I always fear—why should not I?—
The cruel fleeing of your feet.

I am weary of leaves bright and dim,
Of shining box and sombre yew,

Of the horizon's endless rim,
And of all things but you . . . but you. . . .

VII

Above the roof, the sky expands
So blue, so calm;
Above the roof a tall tree stands
And rocks its palm.

The bell that in the sky you see
Chimes sweet and faint,
A bird in the familiar tree
Sings its low plaint.

Dear God, dear God, life glides on there
In tranquil wise.
That peaceful murmur comes from where
The city lies.

O you who stand here full of tears
That flow and flow,
What have you done with the lost years
Of long ago.

[80]

ARTHUR RIMBAUD

VIII

THE SLEEPER OF THE VALLEY

There's a green hollow where a river sings
Silvering the torn grass in its glittering flight,
And where the sun from the proud mountain flings
Fire—and the little valley brims with light.

A soldier young, with open mouth, bare head,
Sleeps with his neck in dewy water cress,
Under the sky and on the grass his bed,
Pale in the deep green and the light's excess.

He sleeps amid the iris and his smile
Is like a sick child's slumbering for a while.
Nature, in thy warm lap his chilled limbs hide!

The perfume does not thrill him from his rest.
He sleeps in sunshine, hand upon his breast,
Tranquil—with two red holes in his right side.

GEORGES RODENBACH

IX

IN SMALL TOWNS

In small towns, in the languid morn and frail
Chimes the far bell, chimes in the sweetness of
Dawn that regards thee with a sister's love,
Chimes the far bell—and then its music pale
Falters upon the roofs like flower on flower,
And on the stairs of gables, dark and deep—
Moist blossoms gathered by the winds that sweep.
The morning music flutters from the tower,
From far away in garlands dry and sere,
Like unseen lilies from an hour that's gone
The petals, cold and pale, drift on and on
As from the dead brow of a perished year.

ÉMILE VERHAEREN

X

Deep in grey dusk the mill turns faltering,
Under a sombre, melancholy sky,
It turns and turns; its earth-hued wheel drifts by
Endlessly feeble and heavy and lingering.

Since dawn its arms in plaintive gesture rise
Heavenward and fall in turn: behold them there
Drooping again deep through the blackening air
And utter silence of a world that dies.

Over the hamlets a cold day foredone
Slumbers; the clouds are weary of voyaging,
To the black woods the massive shadows cling,
To an horizon dead the roads run on.

Some beechen huts, upon the roadway's hem,
Squat in a wretched circle; on their wall
And window a feeble blotch of light lets fall
A copper lamp hanging in one of them.

And in the empty vast of plain and skies
These poor, pinched hovels fix their glances vain
From under lids of broken window-pane
On the old mill that turns and turns and dies.

XI

THE highways run in figure of the rood
Infinitely beyond the wood.
And far away beyond the plains cross-wise
They run into the infinite skies.
Crosses they trace even as they fare
On through the cold and livid air
Where wildly streaming the wind voyages
To the infinite beyond the trees.

The trees and winds like unto pilgrims are,
Sad trees and mad through which the tempests roll,
Trees like long lines of saints coming from far,
Like the long lines of all the dead
For whom the dark bells toll.

O northern trees, astrain for life,
And winds shattering the earth they sweep,
O keen remorse, O human sobs, O bitter strife
Writhing in mortal hearts and ever burrowing
        deep!

[85]

November crouches by the feeble hearth,
And warms his bony fingers at the flame;
O hidden dead without a home or name,
O winds battering the stubborn walls of earth,
Ever hurled back from them and thrown
Out into vastnesses unknown.

O all saints' names scattered in litanies,
O all ye trees below—
O names of saints whose vague monotony is
Infinitely drawn out in memory;
O praying arms that be
Madly as riven branches outstretched wide
To some strange Christ on the horizon crucified.

November here in greyish cloak doth hide
His stricken terror by the ingleside,
And turns his sombre, sudden glance
Across the transept's broken panes of glass
To the tormented trees and winds that pass
Over the blind and terrible expanse.

The saints, the dead, the trees and the wild wind,
The identical and dread processions go

Turning and turning in long nights of snow;
The saints, the dead, the trees and the wild wind,
Blended forever in our memoried hours
When the great hammer blows
That in the echoing bells resonant are
Fling forth their grief to the horizon far
From heights of imprecatory towers.

And near the hearth the dark November lights
With trembling hands of hope for winter nights
The lamp that shall burn for us dim and high;
And full of tears suppliant November prays
To move the dull hearts of the sullen days.

And ever, in the woods without, the iron-coloured
    sky,
Ever the winds, the saints, the dead,
And the processions long and deep
Of trees with tortured boughs outspread
That from the world's end onward sweep.
Across the plains the high roads like the rood
Onward unto the infinite stray,
The highways and their crosses far away
Infinitely beyond the valley and wood.

XII

THE POOR

WITH hearts of poor men it is so:
That they are full of tears that flow,
That they are pale as head-stones white
In the moon light.

And so with poor men's backs it is—
More bent with heavy miseries
Than sagging roofs of brown huts be
Beside the sea.

And it is so with poor men's hands,
Like leaves along autumnal lands,
Leaves that lie sere and dead and late
Beside the gate.

And it is so with poor men's eyes,
Humble and in all sorrow wise,
And like the cattle's, sad and dumb,
When the storms come.

Oh, it is so with the poor folk
That under misery's iron yoke
Have gestures weary and resigned
On earth's far plains of sun and wind.

XIII

LIFE

To exalt thyself all life exalted deem,
Lofty above their lives who dare aspire
Never from sin-wrought woe and quenched desire:
Reality the bitter and supreme
Distils a liquor strong enough and red
To burn the heart and the enraptured head.

Clean wheat from which all tares the tempest
    blew!
Flame chosen from a thousand once so bright
With legendary splendor sunk in night!
Man, set thy foot upon the real and true,
That arduous path unto a distant goal,
Unarmed but for thy lucid pride of soul!

March boldly in thy confidence and straight
At hostile circumstance with stubborn hope,
And with its harshness let thy tense will cope,
Or thy swift wisdom, or thy power to wait,
And deep within thee mark the feeling grow
Of power increasing as the bleak days go.

In love of others find thyself again
Who by that self-same fray exalted are
Toward the same future heard by all afar:
Love thou their equal heart, their equal brain
Who in the days so wild and black and brief
Suffer thy dread, thine anguish and thy grief.

And drink so deeply of this human strife—
Whether a shadow of the cosmic wars
Or golden change amid the wandering stars—
That thou feelst all the thrill and pang of life,
And from thy heart acceptest the stern law
That holds the trembling universe in awe.

JEAN MORÉAS

XIV

O LITTLE FAIRIES . . .

O LITTLE fairies, under your long, long hair
Ye sang to me so sweetly in my sleep,
O little fairies, under your long, long hair,
In the charmed forest of enchantment deep.

Mid the charmed forest's rites of mystery,
Compassionate gnomes, while I was sleeping there,
Offered with kind and honest hands to me
Even while I slept, a sceptre gold and fair.

I have learned since that all is false and vain:
The golden sceptre and the forest lay,
But like a fretful, credulous child I fain
Would in that forest sleep my life away.

What matter that I know it false and vain . . .

XV

THE fennel says: so mad his love,
Your heart it craves the mercy of.
He's coming!   Oh, your hands bestir!—
The fennel is a flatterer.
Dear God, have pity on my soul.

And why, oh why, the daisy saith,
Put all your faith in his light faith?
His heart is hard with lies and hate!—
Daisy, your warning comes too late.
Dear God, have pity on my soul.

The sage-plant says: await him not!
In other arms he has forgot.—
O melancholy sage, I'd wear
Your sad leaves braided in my hair.
Dear God, have pity on my soul.

XVI

1

SAY not: Life is one joyous festival
And a base soul and foolish mind betray—
Nor yet, Black misery is its end and all,
Through courage flagging on an evil way.

Laugh as in Spring the boughs that shake and
    thrill,
Weep like the driven waves that shoreward stream,
Taste every pleasure, suffer every ill,
And say: 'Twas much, though but a shade and
    dream.

2

When the heaviness and void
Of all tragic life we find,
Then the stricken soul is cloyed
Even with tender things and kind.

But a mystic treasure's gleam
Flaming for a little while
Flashes forth as in a dream
And the pallid lips may smile.

And by hope is glorified
All our ancient, dull distress,
As a ragged hedgerow's side
By a young flower's loveliness.

JULES LAFORGUE

XVII

ANOTHER BOOK. . . .

ANOTHER book! How my heart flees
From where these pinchbeck gentry are,
From their salutes and money far,
And all our phraseologies!

Another of my Pierrots gone!
Too lonely in this world was he;
Full of an elegance lunary
The soul that through his quaintness shone.

The gods depart; the fools endure.
Ah, it grows worse from day to day;
My time is up, I take my way
Toward the Inclusive Sinecure.

HENRI DE RÉGNIER

XVIII

SHOWING the whiteness of flesh faint and fair
The hands, the sweet hands that have never spun,
Reveal their jewelled beauty to the sun
And fingers slim that braid the heavy hair.

O hands, you gather beside the waters calm
Great lilies of the river, trembling reed,
And from the neighbouring mountain choose at
    need
Peace of the olive, glory of the palm.

O hands, on the steep river bank you draw
To heal the brow by ancient sin dismayed,
Holy baptismal waters that persuade
Fair forms, new-garmented, to kneel in awe.

O hands of fragrant flesh whose gesture slow
Draws the warm blood to the faint finger-tips,
The weary brows o'er which your beauty slips
Feel heavenly freshness fall like healing snow.

And poets in their red and scarlet girt,
Singing the sorrow of their dream exiled,
Kiss you, dear hands, for being undefiled
By sordid toil, by barren tasks unhurt.

XIX

ON our way to the city of the singing street,
Under the trees whose blossoms are like bridal
    wreaths hung high,
On our way to the city where the squares are sweet
With stillness of tired dances in the rosy evening
    sky,
We met upon our way the maidens of the plain
Who to the fountains fled again
So swiftly that their flight was pain,
And we did pass them by.

The softness of clear heaven dwelt in their sad-
    dened eyes,
The birds of dawn were singing in their voices
    sweet,
The glances of their eyes was gentleness to meet,
And like doves' voices would their tender voices
    rise.
Reserved and sad they sat and watched us all
    depart,
Each guarding in her folded hands her hidden
    heart.

And then we met the dancers on our way,
After their laughing and their tambourines we
    went astray
To lose them in the sombre dusk at a turning of
    the way . . .

We go back to the city of the singing street
To seek our sweethearts under trees and drooping
    flowers,
Where in the silent square the happy chimes are
    sweet,
And even like blossoms shake the belfry towers.

Our hopes shall enter by the open gate
Like fluttering butterflies with outspread wings
    and light,
And with the swallows' flight
Who soar so low and late,
Weary of having crossed so many times the sea—
And toward dark corners and on bright pavements
    we
Shall let our hopes, glad shadows, float in air
Like flower petals marvellously fair
Shed by an April evening upon lovely hair.

XX

A LESSER ODE

> A LITTLE reed has been enough
> To make the high grass shake and thrill,
> The willows tall,
> The meadow wide,
> The brooklet and the song thereof;
> A little reed has been enough
> To make the forest musical.
>
> The passers-by have heard the song
> In the deep evening, in their thoughts
> Whether in silence or in storm,
> Or faint or strong,
> Or near or far. . . .
> The passers-by in their own thoughts
> Hearing it, in their deepest souls
> Will hear it now forevermore—
> A singing reed.
>
> It was enough—
> This little reed once gathered of

Reeds by the fountain where one day
Love came to stay
And see his grave
Face sorrowing—
To make the passing people cry
And grass and water tremble so;
And I who on this reed could blow
He made the very forest sing.

XXI

FEAR not the shadow! Open, lofty gate,
Thy door of bronze, thy door of iron straight.
Deep in a well men have cast down thy key.
Accursèd thou if terror closes thee;
Sever with keen and double-edgèd blade
Hands that have shut thee and that have be-
    trayed.
For under thy dark vault rank forth the feet
Of marching men who never knew retreat,
And in their midst, poised nobly as of old,
Went naked Victory with wings of gold,
And with calm wave of sword their banners
    led.
Upon their lips her ardent kisses bled,
And at their crimson mouths the trumpets rang
With murmur of fierce bees and copper clang!
Wild swarms of war, from hives of armor go,
Pluck from ripe flesh the flowers of death that
    glow,
And if ye to these native walls return,

See that upon my marble threshold burn,
When beneath Victory's wings has passed your
    tread,
Stains of clear blood from sandals steeped in red.

XXII

REST on the shore and take in your two hands,
And let them slip out grain by grain, the sands
Whose paler hue the sun turns into gold;
Then, ere you close your eyes, once more behold
Harmonious ocean and transparent sky,
And when you feel most faintly, by and by,
That in your lightened hand is not a grain,
Consider ere you lift your lids again
That life takes from us and gives evermore
Our fleeting sands to the eternal shore.

XXIII

THE FOREST

HEROIC forest of legend and of dream,
If truth no more thy fabled lies I deem,
And if upon thy paths I meet no more
The weeping princesses I met of yore,
Nor the great, armored knights upon their way
Toward caves where some enchanted beauty lay,
Against whose coming opened, as by fate,
The Keep of Sadness or Love's Orchard-gate—
What matters it?   Hast thou not, without cease,
By turn thy silences and harmonies,
Thy gentle Springs, rich Summers and in them
Thy ripeness with its cloak and diadem?
Hast thou not, happy forest, Autumns rolled
In purple vesture and crowned with gold?
Hast thou not pine serene and oak-tree strong,
And frailer trunks that chant a wind-swept song?
O forest multitudinous as the sea,
Whose perfumes, in their turns, as bitter be,
As sweet as life, as strong, as full of fret. . . .
I came to thee to live and to forget

That once my vision was with fables fed,
For my dream heroes and my gods are dead.
To make thee live, to animate thy shade,
One need but be alone and undismayed,
Nor see in briery hollow and cool brake
Phantoms of dream or sacred creatures wake
To fill thy mystery and solitude.
Art thou not lovelier in thy lonely mood
When none dare stir the greenness of thy night?
For the horned Fauns who danced in loud delight
On the pine cones, on Autumn's foliage dry
Are gone, their hoofs upon the flints that fly
Waken no more the echoes of the glades;
The nymphs have left the springs like fleeting
        shades,
No more their fugitive forms, as water clear,
Misty and empty as the winds appear,
And the tree hides, closing its cloven bark,
The naked Dryad in the silence dark
A prisoner forever.

                    No man's sight
Sees that strange pagan and heraldic fight
Under the branches by the onset torn
Of red-haired Centaur and white Unicorn.

XXIV

CHRYSILLA

Spare me from seeing, goddess, by my bed
When comes the dark hour of the final blow,
Tardy Time cut without regret or woe
A long life's lingering and importunate thread.

Arm rather Love who long desired me dead,
And would his stab supreme might wound me so,
That from the heart he hated forth would flow
My mortal blood staining the earth with red.

But no! At eve let me have vision there
Of my blithe youth, naked and still and fair
And letting rose-leaves upon water drift!

Then I shall hear the fountain's farewell sighs
And without need of sword or arrow swift
Close unto everlasting night mine eyes.

FRANCIS VIELÉ-GRIFFIN

XXV

OTHERS will come across the plain
Near you beside the gate to sit,
And you will smile at all your train
Of lovers, young and exquisite.

They will follow, follow, fleet
Your spring-time and its radiant glow—
Why so very swift their feet?
I was twenty once . . . I know.

All your smiles are now their own,
All your magic youth and strong . . .
What matter they?   For I alone
Poured your sweetness into song.

XXVI

'TIS TIME FOR US TO SAY GOOD NIGHT

'Tis time for us to say good-night,
Fair hours with dreams and roses bright,
Now fled forever with all lost delight. . . .

For thee I waited as one waits for love,
Kept my soul white to dream of when we meet,
Guarded my pureness for thy shoulder sweet
That was to tremble with the kiss thereof.

Whenever from afar I raised mine eyes,
In the young grass rustled thy shadowy shape,
Thy hand did pluck the berry of the grape,
And thy step fluttered like a bird that flies.

Thou wert my hope. Yet now that thou hast
        been,
So fragile in thy beauty and serene,
With love and laughter girt, yet gone away . . .
'Twixt past and future there seems no to-day,
And I have known thee not, I swear, nor seen.

[110]

GUSTAVE KAHN

XXVII

O LOVELY April, rich and bright,
What is thy clarion song to me?
Pale lilac, hawthorne or that golden light
The sun pours through each tree,
If my dear love is far away
And in the Northern gloom must stay.

O lovely April rich and bright;
Meetings are merciless and strange and sweet,
O lovely April rich and bright.
She comes to me.   Thy lilacs white,
Thy sunshine's golden wealth of light
Will charm me when at last we meet,
O lovely April rich and bright.

XXVIII

Hers is a fine and buoyant face;
Yet the small features have a noble trace;
Her flesh's clear grace
Evokes no floral image of delight;
'Tis the flesh's grace, even as through space
The silver of star-light.

Broad is her brow,
White as the temple where but now
Has prayed a faithful worshipper;
Of deepest red the lips of her,
Not purple as the bauble of a king,
But like a bay whose savor has a sting,
A savor with a hint of pain
Which being gathered lives again,
Under our kisses lives again,
Symbol of all faint hope and longing vain.

Soft are her eyes seeing naught save
Seas of a silvery blue and gardens by the wave.

They keep a wide attentive air
Wounded by the music fair
Of sweet songs that rise and fall
In soft speech of that litoral,
Ardent and fragrant by the free
Divine Mediterranean sea.

And when she smiles,
There is clearness on the isles,
The far, white isles from which is borne
When awakens the fresh morn
Radiance of golden sheaves to her,
And of tall grass made tenderer.

XXIX

AGAINST THY KNEES . . .

Against thy knees my pallid brow
Amid the fading roses there;
O lady of Autumn, love me now
Before the black days chill the air.

And move thy gentle hands that seem
To ease my heart, to heal the sting!
Of my ancestral kings I dream,
But thou, lift up thine eyes, and sing.

Soothe me with haunting ditties old,
And songs of valor that has been,
Of kings who in their ruddy gold
Died at the feet of maid and queen.

And when thy liquid voice shall rise
Recalling epic and romance,
And cry even as the bugle cries
Above the harsh swords' flash and dance,

For gentle death I shall be fain
Amid thy roses, O my love,
Too cowardly to win again
The kingdom they have robbed me of.

XXX

THE PROMISE OF THE YEAR

Oh, come with crowns of primroses that in your
    hands are borne,
Maidens weeping for a sister, for a sister dead at
    dawn,
The bells of all the valley ring out for her that's
    gone,
And one sees the shovels flashing in the sunlight
    of the morn.

With baskets of blue violets, come ye maidens all
Who waver at the beech-trees that your sunny
    road runs by,
Because the solemn, priestly words have made your
    hearts feel shy.
Come, for with unseen swallows the sky is musical!

For this is the feast of death and it seems a sabbath
    day;
Many bells are sounding sweet in all the valleys
    wide;

And in the shadows of the lanes the lads have gone
    to hide,
While you must go alone unto her white, white
    tomb to pray.

But in some new year the lads who to-day slip
    out of sight
Will come and tell to all of you the lovely grief
    of love,
And around the merry May-pole one will hear
    your singing of
The roundelays of childhood to salute the starry
    night.

XXXI

THE SEVEN DAUGHTERS OF ORLAMONDE

THE seven daughters of Orlamonde
When the Fay was dead,
The seven daughters of Orlamonde
To seek a doorway fled.

Lit their seven lamps and opened
All the towers of night,
Oh, they opened four hundred halls
And found no light. . . .

And came unto sonorous caves,
Entered falteringly,
And beside a closèd door
Found a golden key.

Saw the ocean through the chinks
Strange and infinite,
And knocked against that closèd door
And dared not open it.

XXXII

I HAVE sought thirty years, my sisters,
Where he hid I sought;
I have walked thirty years, my sisters,
I have found him not.

I have walked thirty years, my sisters,
Weary my footfall;
He is everywhere, my sisters,
And is not at all.

The hour is growing sad, my sisters,
Take my shoes and part;
For as evening wanes, my sisters,
I am sick at heart. . . .

You are very young, my sisters,
Wander on and on;
Take my pilgrim's staff, my sisters,
Seek as I have done. . . .

[119]

RÉMY DE GOURMONT

XXXIII

THE SNOW

SIMONE, white as thy throat the snow I see,
Simone, the snow is white as is thy knee.

Simone, thy hand is cold even as the snow,
Simone, thy heart is cold even as the snow.

The kiss of fire will melt the snow's cold heart,
But thine melts only when we kiss to part.

The snow is sad on the pine-branches there,
Thy brow is sad under its chestnut hair.

In the courtyard thy sister snow sleeps now,
My snow, Simone, and all my love art thou.

XXXIV

Go seeking in the human forest old
The shelter for thy flickering life foretold,
Nor tremble so when evening damps oppress thy
    veins with cold;
Think that the withered flesh no Springtime can
    beguile,
And keep about thy pallid lips the shadow of a
    smile.
Take thou both staff and scrip upon thy ways,
And over the fields follow thou still the trace
Of the tall oxen when to plough they go,
Or children seeking where new flowers, the flowers
    of passion grow.
Perhaps thou wilt find love in that lone land
Or death, or poor men who stretch forth their
    hand
Toward thy heart and wish thee dead;
And thou wilt give them what thou hast, a little
    barley bread;
But they will speak in hostile wise

And at their impure words the tears will start into
    thine eyes.
Weep not! The gods with lofty head,
Though into exile driven the floor of heaven tread.
Thy divine bareness keep from hypocrites apart,
Be ugliness to them, though Beauty's self thou art.

ALBERT SAMAIN

XXXV

EVENING

THE evening's angel passes where flowers
    glow . . .
Our Lady of Dreams now chants her solemn
    hymn;
The sky wherein the hues of day dislimn
Prolongs their faintness into subtle woe.

The evening's angel passes the hearts arow . . .
The impassioned air sways the girls warm and
    slim;
And on the flowers and on the virgins dim
Falls lovely pallor gradual as snow.

The garden's roses have a weary grace,
The soul of Schumann wandering through space
With an immedicable pain is crying. . . .

Somewhere, afar, a gentle child is dying . . .
Place in the book of hours, my soul, a sign,
An angel gathers this sad dream of thine.

XXXVI

PANNYRE OF THE GOLDEN HEELS

On the loud room falls silence like a trance . . .
Pannyre with golden heels comes forth to dance.
A thousand folded veil covers her quite.
With a long trill the silver flutes invite.
She starts, crosses her steps, and with a slow
Movement and sinuous her lithe arms throw
The quivering gauze into a rhythm bizarre,
Which spreads and undulates and floats afar
And like a glittering whirlwind passes by . . .
And she is flower and flame and butterfly!
The rapt eyes follow; there is not a stir.
The fury of the dance enkindles her.
She turns and whirls, swifter she whirls and
    wheels!
The mad flame in the golden torches reels! . . .
Suddenly, in the middle hall, she stops;
The veil, but now a flying spiral, drops
Suspended, marble-calm each long fold lies
Clinging to pointed breasts and polished thighs,
And as through flowing water's silken shine,
Pannyre now flashes—naked and divine.

EDMOND ROSTAND

XXXVII

THE DRUMMER

Early before the unseen cricket-choir
Beats its small cymbal, twangs its little lyre,
When rosy-green the dawning sky's unblurred,
Over the white road of the mountain fair,
Wandereth slowly, playing an olden air,
The drummer, handsome as an antique herd.

Under the pines which sprinkle on the ways
The glittering dews of dawn, he trills and
    plays
On his clear fife, even like a whistling bird.
His drum swings with its ribands green and long.
He goes to sing a gallant morning song
To the lady by whom all his songs are heard.

He breathes into his pipe a merry air,
Beating the time upon his drum from where
The cadences of duller sound are sent.
The little fife of ivory trills and rings,

And the drum follows the bright song it sings
With a monotonous, sad accompaniment.

Drummer of love, lo, how our fate agrees!
I, too, blend sad and merry melodies!
It is my heart—that sombre tone of ill,
Heavier to carry than your drum, my lad!
But always, o'er its plaintive notes and sad,
That mocking pipe, my spirit, whistles still!

FRANCIS JAMMES

XXXVIII

THAT thou art poor I see:
So plain thy little dress.
Dear heart of gentleness,
My grief I offer thee.

But thou art lovelier
Than others; very sweet
Thy fragrant lips to meet
That my slow pulses stir.

And thou art poor and true
And kind as the poor be,
Wouldst have me give to thee
Kisses and roses too.

For but a lass thou art,
And books have made thee dream,
And olden stories deem
That arbors charm the heart,

Roses and mulberries
And flowers of the plain,
Of which the poets feign,
And boughs of rustling trees.

Yes, thou art poor, I see:
So plain thy little dress.
Dear heart of gentleness,
My grief I offer thee.

XXXIX

THE TRAINED ASS

I'M the trained ass, the very ass who can
Startle the learned, counting like a man.
With whip in hand my master makes me climb
An old, cracked tub and balance for a time.
The plaudits of the crowd his zeal enhance.
So down I step and next am forced to dance.
"Where's Paris?" someone asks.   My foot I place
O'er the right spot upon the map of France.
Next: "Ass, survey the circle, face by face,
And stop and with your nodding head point out
Among the audience the most stupid lout."

. . . I obey, quite sure that I make no mistake . . .
My mind, each time he wants to teach me, knows
How the man daily in his ignorance grows.
At night, in the old tent that flaps and jars
Sadly I sleep under the windy sky.
The obsession of knowledge haunts me.   And I try
In my nightmare to count the very stars.

XL

THE CHILD READS AN ALMANAC

THE child reads on; her basket of eggs stands by.
She sees the weather signs, the Saints with awe,
And watches the fair houses of the sky:
The *Goat*, the *Bull*, the *Ram*, et cetera.

And so the little peasant maiden knows
That in the constellations we behold,
Are markets like the one to which she goes
Where goats and bulls and rams are bought and
      sold.

She reads about that market in the sky.
She turns a page and sees the *Scales* and then
Says that in Heaven, as at the grocery,
They weigh salt, coffee and the souls of men.

XLI

You see in Autumn on the telegraph wires
The swallows shiver in a long, dark line.
You feel their little, cold hearts throb and pine.
The very smallest, having seen it not,
To the blue sky of Africa aspires.

. . . Having seen it not, I say.   Even as we
Who long for Heaven in our restless dread.
They perch, watching the air with eager head,
Or fly in little circles hesitantly,
Ever returning to the self-same spot.

'Tis hard to leave the church's sheltering porch!
Hard that it is not warm as in past days!
They are saddened that the old nut-tree betrays
Their faith by the swift falling of its leaves.
The year's young fledglings cannot understand
Dead Spring above which solemn Autumn grieves.

Even thus the soul, wrung by so many woes,
Ere on diviner seas it find its track
And reaches Heaven of the Eternal Rose,
Tries, falters and, before it flees, comes back.

CHARLES GUÉRIN

XLII

BRIGHT HAIR

Amber, ripe rye, or honey full of light,
From combs like Fingal's grotto glittering fair,
Are dull beside my lovely friend's delight
And pride of radiant hair.

When she sleeps near me, happily wearièd,
Beside her sleep in vigil I behold
Her hair under her pallid body spread,
Cradling its white in gold.

When with her folded arm she combs and makes
Patiently smooth the bright skein's tangled mesh,
She throws her head back lightly and she shakes
Gleams on her glimmering flesh.

Her bosom shivers under its caress.
Her slim form stands before the glass and feels
The rippling softness of its longest tress
Against her rosy heels.

HENRY BATAILLE

XLIII

THE WET MONTH

Here in the laundry, through the blurred window-
    pane
I have seen the night of Autumn falling grey . . .
A wanderer passes the ditches full of rain . . .
Traveller, traveller from of old who goest away
Now when the shepherds from the hills descend,
Haste thee! The fires are quenched upon that
    way,
And the doors closed in the land which is thine
    end . . .
The road is empty and the rustle of grass
Comes from so far it frightens us . . . Haste thee;
The lights are out on the old carts that pass . . .
'Tis Autumn sitting in coldness dreamily
On the straw chair in the kitchen hid away . . .
Autumn that in the dead vines chants his lay . . .
This is the moment when unburied men,
White bodies washed between the waves in sleep,
Feel the first chill of shuddering again
And float for shelter into vases deep.

XLIV

THE DEAD GIRL

This girl is dead, is dead in love's old way.

They put her in the earth at break of day.

They laid her lonely in her fine array.

They left her lonely where her lone grave lay.

They came back gaily, gaily with the day.

They sang so gaily, gaily: "None may stay.

The girl is dead, is dead in love's old way."

They went afield, afield as every day . . .

XLV

IMAGES OF OUR DREAMS

THE wooded hill slopes down even unto the
stream; its mirrored image in the tranquil water
lies; rocked in the darker half the deep green
branches seem, and in the azure half the spaces of
the skies.

Here like a skiey pearl a slender shallop glides,
a raft of branches rides not very far away. . . .
Under my very eyes the mist that blinds me hides
and mingles raft and sail into the whelming wave.

Images of our dreams gone down into the
deeps, O aimless raft and sail with watery ports
ahead, blue dream and dark which down the cruel
river sweeps, lost in the wandering wave and
mingled there and dead.

The wooded hill slopes down even unto the
stream. A field of butter-cups shakes on the
other shore. In the sky overcast the pallid flashes
gleam. . . . Ah for our dreams that rise and
perish evermore!

XLVI

IDYLL

1.

EACH time that Eve and Adam meet, he builds
of dreams a Paradise.   This time that landscape
strange and sweet was built by her to please his
eyes.

So for her Adam of thirteen an Eve of twelve
bright Springs did mould a world enchanted
and serene—and during this time I was told

that motherless her years had been, that she
loved tulips red and ripe, that in her "cottage she
was queen," and that her father smoked a pipe.

2.

But on a hidden forest ground the ancient Mystery we found, and God the Ever-seeing knew the
temple veil was rent in two.

We breathed the fragrance of the land, and to our fingers clung the hint of perfume which the leaves of mint in gathering leave on the hand.

"The perfume of our soul's desire. How heady! . . . Here's the storm at last!" She said so sweet and wild. Then passed through the tree tops the forks of fire.

3.

The thunder's peal! Against my side the terror made her cling and hide. And on our knees behold us two . . . saying together: "I love you . . ."

Her tenderness comes back and all her dear caresses I recall, and her blue, ardent eyes adream, her throat and shoulder white as cream.

Fresh air of Spring, why have you made a soul flit back into the shade of these far memories of youth? And of these scenes that fade . . . and fade. . . .

XLVII

BELL OF DAWN

FAINT music of a bell which dawn brings to
my ear, made my heart young again here at the
break of day.

Faint bell-like music which through dewy dawn
I hear ringing so far, so near, changed all I hope
and fear.

What, shall I after this survive my dear-bought
bliss, music by which my soul's far youth recovered
is?

Chiming so far away, so lonely and withdrawn,
O little singing air in the fresh heart of dawn,

you flee, return and ring: seeking like love to
stray, you tremble in my heart here at the break
of day.

Ah, can life ever be of such serenity, so peaceful, mild and fair as is this little air?

So simple yet so sweet as, over meadows borne, this little tune that thrills all the fresh heart of morn?

XLVIII

On the way to Paris, but toward Nemours the white, a bullfinch in the branches sang through the morning-light.

On the way to Orleans, to Nemours flying fleet, a swallow in the heart of day sang above the wheat.

On the way to Flanders, in twilight's gold and grey, far from Nemours the magpie its treasure hid away.

Eastward on to Germany and Russia with harsh cry, far away from this land the crows of evening fly.

But in my lovely garden, in Nemours' sheltered vale, all through the starry hours of night chanted the nightingale.

XLIX

PEGASUS

His pure feet striking sparks of flint that rise,
The mythic beast whose limbs inviolate are
Held by no god or man in rein or bar,
Unto the vast mysteriously flies.

The lessening horse's mane in aureole wise
Becomes, far streaming, an immortal star,
Lustrous in the nocturnal gold like far
Orion glittering in the frosty skies.

And as in days when fair souls and aloof
Drank from the springs struck by his sacred hoof
Their dream of flight into sidereal lands,

Poets who for the reverence lost them weep
Still see in fancy 'neath their feeble hands
The white beast in forbidden heavens leap.

CAMILLE MAUCLAIR

L

PRESENCES

I HAVE seen gentle ladies fade
Into the dusk on soundless feet,
And I have seen their image made
One with the evening, deep and sweet.

Long dead the voices of all these—
Beside some gate shadowy and tall,
Or threshold dim their memories
Dream with the driven leaves of fall.

Even as a poor man makes his bed
In golden Autumn foliage deep,
Lie down, my soul uncomforted,
Amid their memories and sleep.

And to thy very bosom strain
These shadows from the twilight lands,
That their faint fragrance may remain
Within thy heart and on thy hands.

LI

THE MINUTE

"O MY daughter, open the gate!
Someone knocks loud and late!"
"I cannot go and open there,
For at the mirror I smoothe my hair."

"Daughter, open the gate, I say,
A man faints upon the way!"
"I cannot go and look for him yet,
Ribands upon my waist I set."

"Open, O daughter sweet!
I am old, I have dragging feet. . . ."
"I cannot go and watch for him now,
I'm clasping jewels on my brow."

"Perchance the traveller is dead
Out in the cold and wind and dread!"
"If he had been fair I should have guessed:
No thrill has shaken my breast."

HENRI BARBUSSE

LII

THE LETTER

THE clock ticks the slow minutes out,
And the lamp listens as I write.
Soon I shall close mine eyes, no doubt,
And sleep and dream of us to-night.

The soft glow o'er my forehead slips,
Thy voice sounds in my fevered ear . . .
Thy smiling name is on my lips,
And on my hand thy fingers dear.

I feel the charm of yesterday;
Thy poor heart sobs within me now;
And, in this dreaming, who shall say
Whether 'tis I who write, or thou. . . .

FERNAND GREGH

LIII

DOUBT

UPON the topmost branches dies
A last ray of the setting sun;
A glimmer of strange gilding lies
Upon the leaves' vermilion.

From the pale sky the colours fade,
'Tis grey even as grey waters are;
There glide like sudden shafts of shade
The living wings of birds afar.

From all things comes a charm so deep,
So sweet and glad, so void of strife;
Calm as the peacefulness of sleep
Spreads the divinely cosmic life.

The sounds of the far city roll
On fitful winds to my retreat. . . .
Why falls there sudden on my soul
A feeling beyond speaking sweet?

Dear God, how all the sense of doom
Vanishes in the face of things!
How one is like poor men to whom
Some chance a day of feasting brings!

How one adores in childlike mood,
And finds Thee where the shadows fall,
Here in life's holy amplitude,
Thee who, perhaps, art not at all.

PAUL SOUCHON

LIV

ELEGY AT NOON

WHEN in the street at noon the human tide
Sweeps from each house and hurries me aside,
When bars and restaurants with hubbub teem
And from hot plates the vapors heavenward
    steam,
And in the sultry and tumultuous street
Paris sits down at table and to eat—
I think how far in some gold landscape deep
The quiet reaper seeks the shade for sleep,
Drives in his dream the buzzing fly away
That o'er his open lips has come to stray,
And sees on waking, but with eyes closed tight,
Through all his blood roll the resplendent light.

HENRY SPIESS

LV

HANDS

HANDS that in my dream I see
Beckoning me like a star
The brief rose have promised me
And the lily far.

Hands that I have longed to hold
For their gestures magical,
Rings have worn of ancient gold
On their fingers small.

Hands which so I need to bless
Throbbing mouth and fevered eyes,
Sweeter than soft lips caress
And in gentler wise.

When I thought I watched them pass
Ever life the doubt has seen,
And they have, perhaps, alas,
Never truly been.

Yet because I dreamed of them
Long ago and late,
Faithful I have been to them
And I wait and wait. . . .

MAURICE MAGRE

LVI

THE COQUETRY OF MEN

WE too, no less, have all our little arts,
Our pencils, carmines, khols and brushes too,
And in the glass our precious selves we view,
And with gay subtlety arrange our hearts.
The women their complexion scrutinise,
A mark, a blemish, bluish veins that rise,
And skilfully the smallest wrinkle hide.
Thus we contemplate strictly, on our side,
Each form of life that may affect the mind.
We ponder tears and laughter both designed
For the minute and the woman we would please.
We show ourselves bright, sombre or at ease;
We are tricked out so neatly, moulded so
With conscious dreams or some false passion's
    glow,
With such feigned fervor and apparent heat,
Abandon worn like rouge to gull the street,
That in this phantom of disdain or woe
No man the true and hidden heart may know.

Ah, we're alike! Each wears the mask each
    made!
With outstretched arms we wander in the shade
Which we ourselves have woven with our might.
She makes the eye more dark, the throat more
    white,
I cast my thought in forms unknown before.
Each paints with vigor or the heart or face,
One with fair words, one with a pencil's grace—
Both hide their viewless hearts forevermore.

LÉO LARGUIER

LVII

WHEN I AM OLD . . .

WHEN I am old and poet of renown,
And walk with tottering steps and brow bent
    down,
And think of nothing but my verses spread
Like swarms of singing bees about my head—
Where will you be, O my dear love of old?
There in the dusk of life and fame, behold,
I shall be sad, watching the late hours fly,
And follow with an old man's desolate eye
Some lass of twenty trip on footsteps light,
Wearing a pastoral hat with flowers of white,
Just like the hat you wore in other days.
I'll see the inn once more, the wood, the ways,
And all our Autumn journey take again!
I'll people with regret and longing vain
Our village of dead days!   O memory,
So rich in deathless things, yet doomed to die
Although the roses bloom forevermore!
Dear love, dear love, beside my closèd door

Alone I'll sit and watch in gathering damp
Life's barren evening flicker like a lamp.
Upon the garden bench where Autumn sees
The first rain spray, the first leaf in the breeze
Fall like a stricken bird upon the way,
I shall re-live that Autumn day by day—
All! . . . Yet to see in very truth what's gone:
The bracelet on your round arm in the dawn
When you pushed back the small green shutters
        where
The dewy vines shone in the limpid air,
To see again your smile, your forehead's white,
The brown tress hiding it in full moon-light—
Old and renowned, in my dull evenfall,
I would give up my portion in that fame
Which history grants to hearts made musical,
And this poor laurel of a glorious name.

CHARLES VILDRAC

LVIII

IF one were to keep for many years and days,
If one were to keep the lithe and fragrant grace
Of all the hair of women who are dead,
All the blond hair and all the hair of white,
Tresses of gold and coils the hue of night,
And hair of bronze like Autumn's foliage dead,
If one kept these for many years and days,
And wove long veils of them that were to be
Stretched out across the sea,
So many would be stretched over the sea,
So many coils of red, so many tresses bright,
So many silken strands in the sunlight
Would glitter or in billowing breezes play,
That the great birds who fly over the sea
Would often feel, the shadowy birds of grey,
On wing and plumage there,
The kisses ever breathing from this hair,
The many kisses given to this hair,
And then in the great winds blown far away.

[155]

If one were to keep for many years and days,
If one were to keep the lithe and fragrant grace
Of all the hair of women who are dead,
All the blond hair and all the hair of white,
Tresses of gold and coils the hue of night,
And hair of bronze like Autumn's foliage dead,
If one kept these for many years and days,
And twisted ropes of dark and gold and red,
And tethered then
To the great links all earth's imprisoned men,
And bade the prisoners go forth again
Far as the lithe rope led—
The ropes would stretch so far on hill and plain
From all dark thresholds out through sun and
    rain,
That if all prisoners in the world went forth,
Each, wandering South or North,
Would reach his home again.

If Clotho on her busy distaff spun
Instead of my brief life's soon ended thread
The long hair and the heavy of women dead,
Hair dark as rust, hair radiant as the sun,
Hair as the raven's wing,

Or argent as the birches are in Spring,
If Clotho on her busy distaff spun
All tresses of all women who are dead,
I should be lone, so weary and so old,
In a high tower with no thing to behold
And no hope any coming thing to see,
And so bowed down with heavy memory
Of all who had to die,
That I would call for Death—with a great
cry! . . .

GEORGES DUHAMEL

LIX

ANNUNCIATION

FROM the tall mountain's brow
A broken mass of rock
Rolls down the wrinkles of the deep ravine
As though it were a heavy tear of granite.
If it seems to stop for a space
It is but to roll on with a fiercer leap;
A stag set free will not more swiftly reach its cave.
It bounds forth mightily
And plucks out at their very roots
The pines and juniper trees.

Also the wood-cutters toiling upon the slope
Feel a disquietude upon their backs;
And terror freezes their entrails,
While this scourge approaches
Which no man has yet seen.

But I among the heather sunk in deepest peace
Have a heart as calm as is a hooded falcon's,

My skin is clear with blood that nothing can
    affright:
For I know the mountain and the road of ava-
    lanches,
And that the stone may not fall where I am.

But I can point out far below
The trees that it will fell
And the man that it will crush.

ÉMILE DESPAX

LX

Musing I seem upon the glistening space
Among the trees to see
A white bust glimmer on a marble base.
My brother says: 'Tis he.

Brother, though thou love farthest island ways,
Strange sky and ultimate main,
I books and perfect verse and quiet days,
We shall be one through pain.

GENERAL BIBLIOGRAPHY

GENERAL BIBLIOGRAPHY

HURET, JULES: ENQUÊTE SUR L'ÉVOLUTION LITTÉRAIRE. 1891.

MOORE, GEORGE: IMPRESSIONS AND OPINIONS. 1891.

GOURMONT, RÉMY DE: L'IDÉALISME. 1893.

WEIGAND, W.: ESSAYS ZUR PSYCHOLOGIE DER DECADENCE. 1893.

MOCKEL, ALBERT: PROPOS DE LITTÉRATURE. 1894.

WYZÉWA, TÉODORE DE: NOS MAÎTRES. 1895.

LAZARE, BERNARD: FIGURES CONTEMPORAINES. 1895.

DOUMIC, RÉNÉ: LES JEUNES. 1896.

GOURMONT, RÉMY DE: LE LIVRE DES MASQUES. 1896.

VIGIÉ-LECOCQ, E.: LA POÉSIE CONTEMPORAINE. 1897.

BAHR, HERMANN: SKIZZEN UND ESSAYS. 1897.

KAHN, GUSTAVE: PRÉFACE AUX PREMIÈRES POÈMES. 1897.

GOURMONT, RÉMY DE: LE SECOND LIVRE DES MASQUES. 1898.

PELISSIER, GEORGES: ÉTUDES DE LITTÉRATURE CONTEMPORAINE. 1898.

GOURMONT, RÉMY DE: L'ESTHÉTIQUE DE LA LANGUE FRANÇAISE. 1899.

CRAWFORD, VIRGINIA: STUDIES IN FRENCH LITERATURE. 1899.

Souza, Robert de: la poésie populaire et le lyrisme sentimental. 1899.

Symons, Arthur: the symbolist movement in literature. 1899.

Bordeaux, Henry: les écrivains et les mœurs. 1900.

Thompson, Vance: french portraits. 1900.

Gourmont, Rémy de: la culture des idées. 1900.

Mauclair, Camille: l'art en silence. 1900.

Gregh, Fernand: la fenêtre ouverte. 1901.

Brandes, Georg: samlede skrifter. fransk lyrik. vol. vii. 1901.

Hauser, Otto: die belgische lyrik von 1880–1900. 1902.

Charles, J. Ernest: la littérature d'aujourd'hui. 1902.

Kahn, Gustave: symbolistes et décadents. 1902.

Gosse, Edmund: french profiles. 1902.

Beaunier, André: la poésie nouvelle. 1902.

Mendès, Catulle: rapport sur le mouvement poétique français de 1867 à 1900. 1902.

Doumic, Réné: hommes et idées. 1903.

Retté, Adolph: le symbolisme. anecdotes et souvenirs. 1903.

Daxhelet, Arthur: une crise littéraire: symbolisme et symbolistes. 1904.

Bosch, Firmin van den: impressions de littérature contemporaine. 1905.

PELISSIER, GEORGES: ÉTUDES DE LITTÉRATURE ET DE MORAL CONTEMPORAINE. 1905.

ZILLIACUS, EMIL: DEN NYAREN FRANSKA POESIN OCH ANTIKEN. 1905.

GOURMONT, RÉMY DE: PROMÉNADES LITTÉRAIRES. (4 VOLS.) 1905 ff.

LE CARDONEL, GEORGES ET VELLAY, CHARLES: LA LITTÉRATURE CONTEMPORAINE. 1905.

CASELLA, GEORGES ET GAUBERT, ERNEST: LA NOUVELLE LITTÉRATURE. 1895–1905. 1906.

RIMESTAD, CHRISTIAN: FRANSK POESI I DET NITTENDE AAR-HUNDREDE. 1906.

BLUM, LEON: EN LISANT. RÉFLEXIONS CRITIQUES. 1906.

HAMEL, A. G. VAN: HET LETTERKUNDIG LEVEN VAN FRANGRIJK. 1907.

OPPELN-BRONIKOWSKI, F. VON: DAS JUNGE FRANKREICH. 1908.

GRAUTOFF, OTTO UND ERNA: DIE LYRISCHE BEWEGUNG IM GEGENWÄRTIGEN FRANKREICH. 1911.

VISAN, TANCRÈDE DE: L'ATTITUDE DU LYRISME CONTEMPORAIN. 1911.

KEY, ELLEN: SEELEN UND WERKE. 1911.

MERCEREAU, ALEXANDRE: LA LITTÉRATURE ET LES IDÉES NOUVELLES. 1912.

BARRE, ANDRÉ: LE SYMBOLISME. 1912.

HEUMANN, ALBERT: LE MOUVEMENT LITTÉRAIRE BELGE D'EXPRESSION FRANÇAISE DEPUIS 1880. 1913.

LOWELL, AMY: SIX FRENCH POETS. 1915.

BIOGRAPHICAL AND BIBLIOGRAPHICAL
SKETCHES OF THE THIRTY POETS

THE THIRTY POETS

STÉPHANE MALLARMÉ (1842–1898)

was born at Paris of a family of public servants in whom a taste for letters had been traditional for several generations. He completed his preliminary studies at various *lycées* and, having already begun the study of English in order to read Poe, passed some time in England during his twentieth year. The result was a modest independence gained by the teaching of English at colleges and *lycées* first in the South of France, then in Paris from 1862–1892. Already known to men of letters by his verses and translations of Poe, he was revealed to the younger generation by the skilful quotations and praise of J. K. Huysmans in his novel *À Rebours* in 1884. Now began the period of Mallarmé's true fame and wide influence. Unfortunately he survived his retirement from active teaching for only six years. But it is doubtful whether fuller bodied works would have come from his mystical fastidiousness. His admirable work both as a poet and an inspirer of poetry was done.

[169]

CRITICISM AND BIOGRAPHY:

Mauclair, Camille: Stéphane Mallarmé. (n. d.)
Mockel, Albert: Stéphane Mallarmé: Un Héros. 1899.
Wyzéwa, Téodore de: Notes sur Mallarmé. 1886.

THE POETICAL WORKS:

Poésies Complètes. 1887. Vers et Prose, florilège. 1893. Poésies Complètes. 1899.

PAUL VERLAINE (1844–1896)

was born at Metz, the son of a Captain in the French army. The poet's earliest years were passed in various garrison towns. In 1851 Captain Verlaine left the service and settled in Paris. After some preparation Paul entered the old *Lycée Bonaparte*, was made *bachelier ès lettres* in 1862, obtained employment first, curiously enough, with an insurance company, then in several public offices. But soon, especially after the death of his father, he neglected his duties, associated with men of letters, and published his first two volumes which were practically unnoticed. In 1870 he married, became involved in the *Commune*, left Paris, already at odds with his wife and given to drinking, and formed the fatal friendship with Arthur Rimbaud. The two fled in July, 1872, passed together many months of strange wandering in England and Belgium where, in a fit of jealousy, Verlaine shot and wounded Rimbaud. The court at Brussels condemned the poet to two years imprisonment dur-

[170]

ing which time his conversion to Catholicism took place. After his liberation he lived for a year in England, returned to France, taught for a while, engaged in a number of rash and unsuccessful adventures in farming and, having lost his excellent mother in 1886, drifted into that life of passage from hospital to slum and slum to hospital which has become famous as an instance of the union of extreme misery and the highest artistic glory. "A barbarian, a savage, a child," as Jules Lemaître wrote, "but one who heard voices heard by none before."

CRITICISM AND BIOGRAPHY:

Coucke, J.: Paul Verlaine. 1896.

Dullaert, M.: Verlaine. 1896.

France, Anatole: La Vie littéraire. (3e série) 1891.

Lemaître, Jules: Les contemporains. (4e série) 1889.

Lepelletier, Edmond: Paul Verlaine, sa Vie, son Oeuvre. 1907.

Morice, Charles: Paul Verlaine, L'Homme et L'Oeuvre. 1888.

Wätzoldt, S.: Paul Verlaine: Ein Dichter der Decadence. 1892.

THE POETICAL WORKS:

Poèmes saturniens. 1866. Fêtes galantes. 1869. La Bonne Chanson. 1870. Romances sans Paroles. 1874. Sagesse. 1881. Jadis et Naguère. 1884. Amour. 1888. Parallèlement. 1889. Dédicaces.

1889. Femmes. 1890. Bonheur. 1891. Choix de Poésies. 1891. Chansons pour Elle. 1891. Liturgies intimes. 1892. Élégies. 1893. Odes en son honneur. 1893. Dans les limbes. 1894. Épigrammes. 1894. Chair. 1896. Invectives. 1896. Oeuvres Complètes. 5 Vols. 1899–1900. Oeuvres posthumes. 1903.

ARTHUR RIMBAUD (1854–1891)

was born at Charleville in the Ardennes. Though also the son of an army officer he passed his childhood in a sheltered home. Fresh from school the precocious lad ran away, was brought back, escaped a second and a third time, formed the connection with Verlaine and, having recovered from his wounds, travelled in England, Germany, Italy, volunteered with the Carlist army in Spain, with the colonial troups of Holland, deserted and wandered through Java. He returned to Europe, travelled with a circus but finally, helped by his family, departed definitely for the Orient, oblivious of the life of letters, living his literature, merchant in strange lands, purveyor of weapons to the Negus of Abyssinia, dying of a tumor of the knee in Marseilles whither he had gone to visit his family.

CRITICISM AND BIOGRAPHY:

Ammer, K. L. (Eingeleitet von Stefan Zweig): Arthur Rimbaud. Leben und Dichtung. 1907.

Berrichon, Paterne: La Vie de Jean-Arthur Rimbaud. 1897.

Delahaye, Ernest: Rimbaud. 1906.

Rimbaud, Jean-Arthur: Lettres de. 1899.

Verlaine, Paul: Les Poétes Maudits. 1884.

THE POETICAL WORKS:

Poésies complètes. 1895. Oeuvres de Jean-Arthur Rimbaud. 1898.

GEORGES RODENBACH (1855–1898)

was born at Tournai in Belgium of a cultivated family of purely Flemish origin. Early, however, his family moved to Ghent where he attended the college of Sainte-Barbe and the university, taking, in due time, his doctorate in law. In 1876 he went to Paris, engaged in the life of letters, established himself at the Brussels bar in 1885 but returned definitely to Paris two years later. "He will take his rank," wrote Verhaeren, "amongst those whose sadness, gentleness, subtle sentiment and talent fed upon memories, tenderness and silence weave a crown of pale violets about the brow of Flanders."

CRITICISM AND BIOGRAPHY:

Casier, J.: L'Oeuvre poétique de Georges Rodenbach. 1888.

Daxhelet, A.: Georges Rodenbach. 1899.

Guérin, Charles: Georges Rodenbach. 1894.

Le Foyer et les Champs. 1877. Les Tristesses. 1879. Ode à la Belgique. 1880. La Mer élégante. 1881. L'Hiver mondain. 1884. La Jeunesse blanche. 1886. Du Silence. 1888. Le Règne du Silence. 1891. Les Vies encloses. 1896. Le Miroir du ciel natal. 1898.

ÉMILE VERHAEREN (1855–1915)

was born at Saint-Amand near Antwerp of a family of solid Flemish bourgeois, probably of Dutch descent. From the village school at Saint-Amand he proceeded first to Brussels, then to the College of Sainte-Barbe in Ghent where Rodenbach had preceded and Maeterlinck was to follow him. His family destined him to succeed his uncle in the latter's oil refinery. He worked a year in its office, then went to the University of Louvain, completing his studies in the law, forming lettered friendships, joining in the founding of *La Jeune Belgique*. He practised his profession tentatively for a space, but from 1883 on devoted himself wholly to literature. His career now becomes the story of those inner changes and adventures analysed in the text and of the growth of his fame first in Belgium and France, later in Germany, finally in England and America. He died from injuries sustained in an accident.

Criticism and Biography:

Bazalgette, Léon: Émile Verhaeren. 1907.

Boer, Julius de: Émile Verhaeren. 1908.

Buisseret, Georges: L'Évolution Idéologique de Émile Verhaeren. 1910.

Gauchez, M.: Émile Verhaeren. 1908.

Guilbeaux, Henri: Émile Verhaeren. 1908.

Schellenberg, E. A.: Émile Verhaeren. 1911.

Schlaf, Johannes: Émile Verhaeren. 1905.

Zweig, Stefan: Émile Verhaeren. German and French editions: 1910: English, 1914.

THE POETICAL WORKS:

Les Flammandes. 1883. Les Moines. 1886. Les Soirs. 1887. Les Débacles. 1888. Les Flambeaux noirs. 1890. Au bord de la Route. 1891. Les Apparus dans mes Chemins. 1891. Les Campagnes hallucinées. 1893. Almanach. 1895. Les Villages illusoires. 1895. Les Villes tentaculaires. 1895. Les Heures Claires. 1896. Les Visages de la Vie. 1899. Petites Légendes. 1900. Les Forces tumultueuses. 1902. Toute la Flandre. Les Tendresses premières. 1904. Les Heures d'Après-midi. 1905. La Multiple Splendeur. 1906. Toute la Flandre. La Guirlande des dunes. 1907. Toute la Flandre. Les Héros. 1908. Toute la Flandre. Les Villes à Pignons. 1909. Les Rythmes souverains. 1910. Les Heures du Soir. 1911. Toute la Flandre. Les Plaines. 1912. Les Blés mouvants. 1912.

JEAN MORÉAS (1856–1910)

was born at Athens, a descendant of two Greek families illustrious in peace and war. His real name, too cumbersome for a French man of letters, was Papadiamantopoulos. His education at Athens was wholly French and, as a very young man, he took up his residence in Paris. His life was devoted wholly to literature. Having visited various German cities, as well as Italy, he made his last visit to his native country in 1897. From then on his preoccupation with poetry was complete.

CRITICISM AND BIOGRAPHY:

　　Gourmont, Jean de: Jean Moréas. 1905.
　　Maurras, Charles. Jean Moréas. 1891.
　　France, Anatole. La Vie littéraire. (4e série.)
　　　1892.

THE POETICAL WORKS:

　　Les Syrtes. 1884. Les Cantilènes. 1886. Le
　　Pèlerin passioné. 1891. Ériphyle, poème suivi de
　　Quatre Sylves. 1894. Les Stances (Ier et IIe
　　livres). 1899. Les Stances. (IIIe, IVe, Ve, et
　　VIe livres). 1901.

JULES LAFORGUE (1860–1887)

was born at Montevideo where his father was tutor. The boy was placed early in the *lycée* at Tarbes where he remained until the family returned to Europe and settled in Paris. Completing his education in 1879 Laforgue formed his momentous friendship with M. Gustave Kahn. There followed years of severe literary poverty until in 1881, partly through the influence of M. Paul Bourget, Laforgue was appointed reader to the Empress Augusta at Berlin. In 1886 he left this post, married a young Englishwoman whom he had met in Berlin, but already fallen into consumption survived this event only one year.

CRITICISM AND BIOGRAPHY:

> Dufour, Médéric: L'Esthétique de Jules Laforgue. 1905.
>
> Mauclair, Camille: Jules Laforgue, Essai. Avec une Introduction de Maeterlinck. 1896.

THE POETICAL WORKS:

> Les Complaintes. 1885. L'Imitation de Notre-Dame la Lune. 1886. Le Concile féerique. 1886. Derniers Vers. 1890. Poésies Complètes. 1894.

HENRI DE RÉGNIER (born 1864)

is descended from a family distinguished even amid the older nobility of France. From his native place Honfleur, the family moved to Paris in 1874 and Régnier passed through the College Stanislas where he had already written. He studied law but began publishing verse almost immediately. He took a vital part in the founding of the Symbolist movement, sought out Verlaine and was Mallarmé's closest intimate among the younger men. In 1896 he married Mlle. Marie de Hérédia, second daughter of the author of *Les Trophées* and herself a poet of distinction. M. de Régnier, almost as celebrated to-day in prose fiction as in verse, has never had to wait for recognition. It came to him early: it gave him the opportunity of undivided devotion to art. He is by common accord the representative French poet of his time.

CRITICISM AND BIOGRAPHY:

Gourmont, Jean de: Henri de Régnier et son oeuvre. 1908.

Léautaud, Paul. Henri de Régnier. 1904.

Mauclair, Camille: Henri de Régnier. 1894.

THE POETICAL WORKS:

Lendemains. 1885. Apaisement. 1886. Sites. 1887. Épisodes. 1888. Poèmes anciens et ro-manesques. 1890. Tel qu'en Songe. 1892. Arethuse. 1895. Les Jeux rustiques et divins. 1897. Les Médailles d'Argile. 1900. La Cité des Eaux. 1902. La Sandale ailée. 1906. Le Miroir des Heures. 1911.

FRANCIS VIELÉ-GRIFFIN (born 1864)

is a native of Norfolk, Virginia. He was taken to France in his boyhood, received a wholly French education and printed verse in his adopted tongue as early as 1885. He was one of the strongest theoretical spirits in the Symbolist movement, edited one of its early reviews, fought for it and has remained true to it ever since.

A wide reading of the criticism and poetry of his period serves to heighten one's sense of his wide influence and of the esteem in which he and his work are held by his fellow craftsmen in France.

CRITICISM AND BIOGRAPHY:

Henri de Régnier: Francis Vielé-Griffin. 1894.

THE POETICAL WORKS:

Cueille d'Avril. 1886. Les Cygnes. 1887. Joies. 1889. Les Cygnes. Nouveaux Poèmes. 1892. La Chévauchée d'Yeldis et autres poèmes. 1893. Πάλαι, poèmes. 1894. La Clarté de Vie. 1897. La Partenza. 1899. L'Amour sacré. 1903. Plus loin. 1906. La Lumière de la Grèce. 1912. Voix d'Ionie. 1914.

GUSTAVE KAHN (born 1859)

is a native of Metz, of Jewish birth. He studied at the *École des Chartes* and the *École des langues orientales* and spent four years of his early manhood in Africa. In 1885 he returned to Paris, resumed his literary work and, a year later, founded *La Vogue*, the little review which saw the birth of free verse. Almost at the same time he edited (with Moréas and Paul Adam) *Le Symboliste* and in 1889 revived *La Vogue*. These details are important in the history of French poetry. M. Kahn's claims as the founder of the free verse movement have been disputed. But the movement first found expression through him and he gave it its complete critical theory. Up to 1897 he devoted himself to poetry. Since he has written fiction but chiefly criticism of a very subtle and penetrating kind.

CRITICISM AND BIOGRAPHY:

Fénéon, Félix: Kahn. (Les Hommes d'aujourd'-hui.) n. d.

Randon, G.: Gustave Kahn.

THE POETICAL WORKS:

Les Palais Nomades. 1887. Chansons d'amant. 1891. Domaine de Fées. 1895. La Pluie et le Beau Temps. 1895. Limbes de Lumière. 1895. Le Livre d'Images. 1897.

STUART MERRILL (born 1863)

is a native of Hempstead, Long Island. His childhood and boyhood were passed in Paris and at the *Lycée Condorcet* he had as fellow-students half a dozen of the future Symbolists. In 1885 he returned to New York, studied law at Columbia, and in 1890, published through Harper & Brothers a series of translations from contemporary French literature called *Pastels in Prose*. He returned to France, devoted himself to poetry and Socialistic work and wrote articles on French literature for the New York *Times* and *Evening Post*. Neither as a social reformer—often through the medium of the arts—nor as a poet of ever deeper and riper power

—though in a foreign tongue—has M. Merrill ever received the recognition in his native country which is his due.

THE POETICAL WORKS:

Les Gammes. 1887. Les Fastes. 1897. Petits Poèmes d'Automne. 1895. Les Quatre Saisons. 1900.

MAURICE MAETERLINCK (born 1862)

It would be superfluous to give a sketch of Maeterlinck here. For a full discussion of his dramatic works with bibliographical material the reader is referred to: Lewisohn: *The Modern Drama* (2nd Ed.) 1917. Maeterlinck abandoned poetry early. What he did write in verse is interesting as contributing the peculiar Maeterlinckian note also to modern French poetry.

THE POETICAL WORKS:

Serres chaudes. 1889. Douze Chansons. 1896.

RÉMY DE GOURMONT (1858–1915)

was born at the chateau de la Motte at Bazoches-en-Houlme. On his father's side he came of a family of famous printers and engravers of the Fifteenth and Sixteenth Centuries, on his mother's side he was a collateral descendant of Malherbe. As a youth he was an employé of the *Bibliothèque nationale.* An article of his in the *Mercure de France* offended official patriotism and he was dismissed. He now gave himself up to his vast intellectual labors as poet, critic, dramatist, philosopher, biologist, novelist, grammarian, etc., contributing to French, German, Austrian, North and South American reviews and publishing dozens of volumes of an extraordinary intellectual richness, subtlety and stylistic charm. A great man of letters, if a poet of but secondary rank.

CRITICISM AND BIOGRAPHY:

Querlon, Pierre de: Rémy de Gourmont. 1903.
Vorluni, Giuseppe: Rémy de Gourmont. 1901.

THE POETICAL WORKS:

Hiéroglyphes. 1894. Les Saintes du Paradis. 1899. Oraisons mauvaises. 1900. Simone, poème champêtre. 1901. Divertissements. (A reprint of the contents of the earlier volumes together with: Paysages spirituels, Le Vieux Coffret and La Main. 1914.

ALBERT SAMAIN (1858–1900)

was the son of a family of small bourgeois of Lille. Losing his father at fourteen he had to leave school and passed difficult years in commerce. The government service first at home, later (1880) in Paris brought relief and increased leisure. His shy and frugal genius came to a rather late maturity, and when at last a measure of fame was his, bereavement and ill health had already broken him.

CRITICISM AND BIOGRAPHY:

Bersaucourt, Albert de: Conférence sur A. Samain. 1907.

Bocquet, Léon: Albert Samain, sa Vie, son Oeuvre. 1905.

THE POETICAL WORKS:

Au Jardin de L'Infante. 1893. Aux Flancs du Vase. 1898. Le Chariot d'Or. 1901.

EDMOND ROSTAND (born 1868)

For a detailed account of Rostand the reader may again be referred to Lewisohn: *The Modern Drama* (2nd Ed.) 1917. M. Rostand is curiously below his highest level when not using the medium of drama. But his inclusion here was necessary to mark an important element in modern French poetry.

THE POETICAL WORKS:

Les Musardises.

FRANCIS JAMMES (born 1868)

is a native of Tournay (Hautes-Pyrénées) a thorough Frenchman of the South. His grandfather emigrated to South America, his father was born there. After the latter's early death the poet, having been a collegian at both Pau and Bordeaux settled with his mother at Orthez where he has since lived and which he has made famous by his verse. He published first in locally printed pamphlets. One of these attracted the attention of the *Mercure de France* in 1893. The reviewer, observing a dedication to Hubert Crackanthorpe, reasoned that Jammes must be a printer's error for James. So humble were the beginnings of a poet who soon conquered a very distinct and secure fame for himself. His personal beliefs and tastes and history need hardly any commentary beyond his verses.

THE POETICAL WORKS:

Four pamphlets of verse, all printed at Orthez between 1891 and 1894. Un Jour, poème dialogué. 1896. La Naissance du Poète. 1897. De l'Angelus de l'Aube à l'Angelus du Soir. 1898. Le Deuil des Primevères. 1901. Le Triomphe de la Vie. 1902. L'Église habillée de feuilles. 1906. Clairières dans le Ciel. 1906. Pensée des Jardins. 1906. Poèmes mesurés. 1908. Les Géorgiques Chrétiennes. 1912.

CHARLES GUÉRIN (1873–1907)

was born of a family of wealthy manufacturers of Luneville. He studied at Nancy, lived alternately at Luneville and Paris and spent much time in Germany and Italy. His reputation was established early, but a crisis of the soul which made him a Catholic seemed to rob him of lyrical spontaneity. He was aware of this fact which lends pathos to some of his last verses.

THE POETICAL WORKS:

Joies grises. 1894. Sonnets et un Poème. 1897.
Le Coeur Solitaire. 1898. Le Semeur des Cendres.
1901. L'Homme Intérieur. 1905.

HENRY BATAILLE (1872)

is a native of Nimes. His single volume of verse is of
extraordinary originality and earned for him a place in
Gourmont's *Livre des Masques*. It is unfortunate that
the writing of his vigorous but by no means first rate
plays has permitted him to add but a few new poems in
the second edition of his original collection.

THE POETICAL WORKS:

La Chambre Blanche. 1895. Le Beau Voyage.
1904.

PAUL FORT (born 1872)

is a native of Rheims. Of his origin or family little
information is available at present. As a youth of
eighteen he founded the *Théâtre d'Art* in opposition to
the dominance of Naturalism and presented *The Cenci*
and pieces by Verlaine, Maeterlinck, Gourmont, etc. In
1893 the theatrical venture collapsed and M. Fort turned
definitely to poetry. His productivity since then has been
enormous. To live and write the sixteen volumes of the
Ballades françaises in twenty years is, in itself, a sufficient
biography.

Ballades françaises. 1897. Montagne. Ballades françaises. IIe Série. 1898. Le Roman de Louis XI. Ballades françaises. IIIe Série. 1899. Les Idylles Antiques. Ballades françaises. IVe Série. 1900. L'Amour marin. Ballades françaises. Ve Série. 1900. Paris Sentimental ou le Roman de nos vingt ans. Ballades françaises. VIe Série. 1902. Les Hymnes de feu. Ballades françaises. VIIe Série. 1903. Coxcomb ou l'homme tout nu tombé du Paradis. Ballades françaises. VIIIe Série. 1906. Île de France. Ballades françaises. IXe Série. 1908. Montcerf. Ballades françaises. Xe Série. 1909. La Tristesse de l'homme. Ballades françaises. XIe Série. 1910. L'Aventure Éternelle. Ballades françaises. XIIe Série. 1911. Montlhéry-La-Bataille. Ballades françaises. XIIIe Série. 1912. Vivre en Dieu. Ballades françaises. XIVe Série. 1912. Chansons Pour se consoler d'Être Heureux. Ballades françaises. XVe Série. 1913. Les Nocturnes. Ballades françaises. XVIe Série. 1914.

HENRI BARBUSSE (born 1874)

is a native of Asnières. He is a dramatic critic, a distinguished journalist and novelist. His early poems, charming in themselves, take on an added interest now as coming from the author of *Le Feu*.

THE POETICAL WORKS:
Pleureuses. 1895.

PIERRE LOUYS (born 1870)

is a native of Paris and the son of a distinguished house. His education was learned and, unlike the majority of modern French poets, he is a scholar in the technical sense. His work as a man of letters is almost wholly the result of the influence of his Greek studies upon his ardent temperament. His novel *Aphrodite* (1896) made his reputation international: his pseudo-versions of Greek poetry have deceived the learned. His publication of verse in which he speaks in his own person has been limited.

CRITICISM AND BIOGRAPHY:
Gaubert, Ernest: Pierre Louys. 1904.
Wilamowitz-Moellendorf, Ulrich von: Pierre Louys. Göttingische Gelehrte Anzeigen. 1896.

THE POETICAL WORKS:
Astarté. 1891. Les Poésies de Méléagre. 1893. Les Chansons de Bilitis. 1894.

CAMILLE MAUCLAIR (born 1872)

a native of Paris and of Jewish origin is one of the most fertile minds of modern France. An admirable poet and story writer he has achieved his highest distinction as a critic of literature, of thought and of painting.

CRITICISM AND BIOGRAPHY:

Aubry, G.-Jean: Camille Mauclair. 1905.

THE POETICAL WORKS:

Sonatines d'Automne. 1895. Le sang parle. 1904.

FERNAND GREGH (born 1873)

is a native of Paris. His rise to fame because one of his poems was mistaken by good judges for Verlaine's was sudden. But he has known how to sustain it and his work commends itself, more than that of most of the younger men, to the acknowledged chiefs of French criticism, Faguet and Lanson.

THE POETICAL WORKS:

La Maison de l'Enfance. 1897. La Beauté de vivre. 1900. La Clarté humaine. 1904. L'Or des Minutes. 1905. La Chaîne éternelle. 1910.

PAUL SOUCHON (born 1874)

is a native of Laudun on the Rhône. He is practically the only modern French poet of immediate peasant descent, which may account for the clearness, the sobriety, the realism of his work. He has written—an uncommon thing in this age—only verse.

THE POETICAL WORKS:

Les Élévations poétiques. 1898. Nouvelles Éléva-

tions poétiques. 1901. Élégies Parisiennes. 1902.
La Beauté de Paris. 1904.

HENRY SPIESS (1876)

is a native of Geneva and an interesting representative of
the French literary movement in West Switzerland. He
is a lawyer and started out with a whimsical but poetical
interpretation of his profession.

THE POETICAL WORKS:
Rimes d'Audience. 1903. Le Silence des Heures.
1904. Chansons captives. 1910.

MAURICE MAGRE (born 1877)

is a native of Toulouse and strove, for a time, to make
his native city a centre of literature and criticism. He
then abandoned it for Paris where his productivity in
later years has been largely in the direction of poetic
drama. (*Les Belles de nuit.* 1913).

THE POETICAL WORKS:
Éveils. 1895. La Chanson des Hommes. 1898.
Le Poème de la Jeunesse. 1901. Les Lèvres et le
Secret. 1906.

LÉO LARGUIER (born 1878)

is a native of La Grand' Combe in the Cévennes. Almost alone among the younger poets he has kept clear
of Symbolism and carries on consciously and with an

air of magnificence the tradition of Lamartine and Hugo. Forced, apparently, into several sorts of superior hack-work (*Les Grands Écrivains à travers les Grands Villes*) he has not, like many of his contemporaries, abandoned his admirable poetic work.

THE POETICAL WORKS:

La Maison du Poète. 1903. Les Isolements. 1906. Jacques, poème. 1907. Orchestres. 1914.

CHARLES VILDRAC (born 1882)

a native of Paris, is one of the leaders of the latest movement—a subtle thinker, a remarkable experimenter in verse.

THE POETICAL WORKS:

Poèmes. 1905. Images et Mirages. 1908. Le Livre d'Amour. 1910. Découvertes. 1912.

GEORGES DUHAMEL (1882)

is, like his brother-in-law Vildrac, a Parisian and an insurgent, and collaborated with him in the most definite statement of the achievement and principles of the new school: *Les Poètes et La Poésie.* 1914.

THE POETICAL WORKS:

Des Légendes, des Batailles. 1907. L'Homme en Tête. 1909. Selon ma Loi. 1910. La Lumière. 1911.

EMILE DESPAX (1881)

is a native of Dax, a man of liberal education, a government official, an excellent example of the more traditional poetic workman of France.

THE POETICAL WORKS:

Au Seuil de la Lande. 1902. La Maison des Glycines. 1905.

INDEX OF THE FIRST LINES IN
FRENCH AND ENGLISH

INDEX OF FIRST LINES

[195]

D'autres viendront par la pré, 109
> *Others will come across the plain*

De ses quatre pieds purs faisant feu sur le sol, 142
> *His pure feet striking sparks of flint that rise*

Du coté de Paris, 141
> *On the way to Paris*

Du front de la montagne, 158
> *From the tall mountain's brow*

En allant vers la Ville où l'on chante aux terasses, 99
> *On our way to the city of the singing street*

Encore un livre : ô nostalgies, 96
> *Another book!   How my heart flees*

En province, dans la langueur matutinale, 82
> *In small towns, in the languid morn and frail*

Héroique forêt de légende et de songe, 106
> *Heroic forest of legend and of dream*

Il est ainsi de pauvres coeurs, 88
> *With hearts of poor men it is so*

Il faut admirer tout pour s'exalter soi-même, 90
> *To exalt thyself all life exalted deem*

Il meurt sur les plus hautes branches, 146
> *Upon the topmost branches dies*

Il pleut.   Je rêve.   Et je crois voir entre les arbres, 160
> *Musing, I seem upon the glistening space*

J'ai cherché trente ans, mes soeurs, 119
> *I have sought thirty years, my sisters*

J'ai vu les femmes qui s'en vont, 143
I have seen gentle ladies fade

J'allais par des chemins perfides, 77
Sad and lost I walked where wide

Je fais souvent ce rêve étrange et pénétrant, 74
Often this strange and poignant dream is mine

Je sais que tu es pauvre, 127
That thou art poor I see

Je suis l'âne savant, celui même qui étonne, 129
I'm the trained ass, the very ass who can

Je t'écris et la lampe écoute, 145
The clock ticks the slow minutes out

La colline boisée vient border la rivière, 136
The wooded hill slopes down even unto the stream

L'ambre, le seigle mûr, le miel plein de lumière, 133
Amber, ripe rye or honey full of light

La lune s'attristait. Des seraphins en pleurs, 73
The moon grew sad. The tear-stained seraphim

Le ciel est, par-dessus le toit, 80
Above the roof the sky expands

L'enfant lit l'almanach près de son panier d'œufs, 130
The child reads on. Its basket of eggs stands by

Le moulin tourne au fond du soir, très lentement, 83
In deep grey dusk the mill turns faltering

Le piano que baise une main frêle, 78
The key-board which frail fingers gently stir

Les grand'routes tracent des croix, 85
The highways run in figure of the rood

[197]

[198]

On voit, quand vient l'automne, aux fils télégraphiques, 131
   You see in Autumn on the telegraph wires

Par les vitres grises de la lavanderie, 134
   Here, in the laundry, through the blurred window-
   pane
Porte haute! ne crains point l'ombre, laisse ouvert, 103
   Fear not the shadow!   Open, lofty gate

Quand de la tragique vie, 94
   When the heaviness and void

Si l'on gardait, depuis des temps, des temps, 155
   If one were to keep for many years and days
Simone, la neige est blanche comme ton cou, 120
   Simone, white as thy throat the snow I see
Sous vos longues chevelures, petites fées, 92
   O little fairies, under your long, long hair

Un coup de tonerre!   Et l'effroi, 138
   The thunder's peal!   Against my side
Un petit roseau m'a suffit, 101
   A little reed has been enough

Va cherche dans la vieille forêt humaine, 121
   Go seeking in the human forest old
Venez avec des couronnes de primevères dans vos mains,
   116
   Oh, come with crowns of primroses that in your
   hands are borne

[199]